THE BIBLE BASIS
OF MISSIONS

By

ROBERT HALL GLOVER, M.D., F.R.G.S.

Home Director Emeritus for North America of the China Inland Mission.
Author of The Progress of World-Wide Missions, *etc.*

Introduction by

SAMUEL M. ZWEMER, D.D., LL.D.

Professor Emeritus of History of Religion and Christian Missions,
Princeton Theological Seminary. Editor, The Moslem World

BIBLE HOUSE OF LOS ANGELES

927 So. Westmoreland Avenue
Los Angeles 6, California

The Bible Basis of Missions
PRINTED IN THE UNITED STATES OF AMERICA

To

My Former Students

who faithfully serve on the far-flung

mission fields of the world,

this book is affectionately inscribed

PREFACE

THE author is aware that there already exists a fair-sized library of books which deal with the subject of the missionary character and teaching of the Bible. Quite a number of these are on his own book shelves and have been read with true appreciation of their scholarly character and high value. He has therefore had to face the question, which will doubtless arise in other minds as well, whether there is any need for another book on this theme. His conclusion, reached only after much thought and prayer, was that there still is room for a treatment of the subject from a point of view, and along a line, somewhat different from that of these other volumes.

This conclusion has seemed to be confirmed by repeated requests received from members of his former Missions classes in several Bible institutes, and also from others who have attended lectures on the subject in two seminaries and various Bible conferences, that the material there given might be made available in book form.

It has not been easy to find time, in the midst of other duties, for this added task, but little by little the chapters which follow have been written and are now sent forth. No pretense is made that they constitute a fully rounded discussion of the vital subject with which they deal, and the author is keenly conscious of the limitations and imperfections of his presentation of it. His only claim is that what he has written is prompted by a deep concern that a truer conception of the vital place of missions in the divine purpose and plan be somehow imparted to the Church of today, leading to a new and more worthy effort to carry forward to completion the task committed by Christ to His Church on earth, at its birth, and which constitutes the very object of its existence, namely, giving the Message of Salvation to all mankind.

The author wishes to pay grateful tribute to Mrs. Jeannette Rorke, his former devoted and efficient secretary, for her valuable services, so generously given, in typing and preparing for publication the entire manuscript of this book, and also to Miss Mildred Cook, a former gifted student of his, for her painstaking and most helpful editorial assistance.

R. H. G.

Philadelphia, Pa.
December 1945

INTRODUCTION

WE ARE confident that the Christian public will welcome this new study of an old theme, the Bible and Missions. Although, as the author states in his Preface, a goodly number of books have been written on the subject, there are at least two valid reasons for commending this Biblical approach—reasons apt to be forgotten in a day when the economic and social aspects of the Gospel message are sometimes overemphasized.

First, this study has an explicit theology. We have had manuals on missions that stressed sociology, psychology, and even ethics, but left out theology except in tabloid form. If evangelical Christianity is reducible, as one author states, "to a successful communication of a valuable experience," we need no theology of missions. But the New Testament makes perfectly clear that the aim of Christian missions is the fulfillment of a divine command and an eternal divine purpose in the witness to the fact of Jesus Christ. The evangelization of the world is not a human but a divine project. The word of the Cross was the message of the apostles; the power of the Cross was their motive, and the glory of the resurrection was their inspiration and hope. Missions both in the Old Testament promises and prophecies and in their New Testament power and victory bear not a worldly but an otherworldly character. Atonement for sin and victory over sin always end in victory over death. The apostles preached Christ and His resurrection, which is the pledge of ours. Whatever may be said of the early church, this is undoubtedly true, that its back was toward the world and its face toward the coming of the Lord. Its course was steered not only by the chart of its faith but also by the polestar of its hope.

Second, this study deals with a basic philosophy. The subject is approached from the same angle as that taken by Dr. Hendrik Kraemer of the Madras Conference in his volume, *The Christian Message in a Non-Christian World*. The view of both Dr. Glover

7

and Dr. Kraemer is at the antipodes of *Re-Thinking Missions* and the other book of Professor William E. Hocking, *Living Religions and a World Faith*. Both stand in awe before the fact of a final revelation and the unique finality of Jesus Christ.

The only missionary motive that is not smitten to pieces by the atomic bombs of rationalism and neo-paganism in our day is the apostolic mandate of the New Testament, with all of its implications and sanctions. These are set forth in the present popular study of missions. To recommend Christianity merely as the bringer of a higher culture, or to offer Asia and Africa a larger share than they now have in Western civilization and philosophy, is a hopeless task, for it is to be observed that the two most scientifically progressive and most literate nations of Europe and Asia have plunged the world into chaos and the utter barbarism of modern warfare.

When the foundations of morals and faith are destroyed, what can the righteous do? They can only arise in God's strength to build more securely than ever upon the Rock of Ages. We must go back to the Bible itself for our missionary motive, our message and our dynamic. Only in the Bible do we find the origin and the goal of the enterprise.

The Biblical method is the way recommended and illustrated in these pages. Each chapter finds its authoritative note in the Word of God. All are based and buttressed not on a new philosophy of missions or on the type of ecumenics that loses itself in a worldview apart from a deep sense of the world-need of the Gospel. According to Dr. Glover's conviction, the Word of God is the only rule of faith and practice in the missionary enterprise.

We have read the manuscript of these pages with joy to find virility of thought coupled with clear vision and the handling of difficult themes with sanity as well as sanctity. The author has had long experience in China as a practicing missionary, and at home in wide and wise missionary administration. He is no theorist but a man of practical judgment. When he speaks of the Holy Spirit and missions he deals with facts witnessed personally on the mission field. When he tells of the supreme place of the pastor in missions, he knows whereof he speaks. The chapter on "Christ's

Return and Missions" is sober and strong, and it contains a warning for those whose eschatology may lead to disappointment—those who, intent on minor issues, are like the man who spent so much effort to understand the timetables at the railway station that he missed the train.

In the interest of the great cause of world-evangelization, here is the book for the hour. It is written for the day in which we live, and written by one who has fought a good fight and kept the faith. Open its pages and judge for yourself. We believe this book belongs to the third class in Francis Bacon's category: "Some books are to be tasted, others to be swallowed, and some few to be chewed and digested."

SAMUEL M. ZWEMER

New York City
December 1945

CONTENTS

CHAPTER   PAGE

I   THE BIBLE AND MISSIONS   13
The Missionary Character of the Scriptures

II   THE CHURCH AND MISSIONS   31
World-Evangelization the Church's Supreme Aim and Task

III   THE PASTOR AND MISSIONS   43
The Home Pastor's Strategic Relation to World-Evangelization

IV   THE HOLY SPIRIT AND MISSIONS   55
The Divine Enduement and Leadership in Missions

V   THE APOSTLE PAUL AND MISSIONS   72
Salient Features of New Testament Missions Exemplified in Paul

VI   CHRIST'S RETURN AND MISSIONS   96
The True Perspective and Goal of Missionary Effort

VII   MEN AND MISSIONS   125
The Essential Elements of a Missionary Call

VIII   MONEY AND MISSIONS   142
Bible Light on Missionary Stewardship

IX   PRAYER AND MISSIONS   165
The Vital Place of Missionary Intercession

X   THE "LITTLE LAD" AND MISSIONS   187
Feeding the Multitude—a Missionary Parable

11

I

THE BIBLE AND MISSIONS

The Missionary Character of the Scriptures

It is not sufficient to be able to say that we are "interested in missions," nor even that we are taking some part in the promotion of missions. A good deal of missionary interest and effort falls short of being satisfactory, because it rests upon an altogether inadequate conception of what the missionary enterprise really is. Mere pity for the people of mission lands, called forth by some heart-moving tale of dire need or some instance of cruel suffering, is not enough, commendable though this may be. Something deeper and broader is needed to constitute a solid foundation for worthy and enduring missionary effort.

The missionary enterprise is no human conception or undertaking, no modern scheme or invention, no mere philanthropy even of the finest kind. It did not originate in the brain or heart of any man, not even of William Carey, or the apostle Paul. Its source was in the heart of God Himself. And Jesus Christ, God's great Missionary to a lost world, was the supreme revelation of His heart and expression of His love.

The one great fact in which all true thoughts of God must find their root is the fact of John 3:16, that "God so loved the world, that he gave his only begotten Son, that whosoever believeth in him should not perish, but have everlasting life." This verse is commonly regarded as the central text of the New Testament, the very heart of the Gospel. For this reason it is also the central missionary text. Along with it several other texts naturally associate themselves: "For God sent not his Son into the world to condemn the world; but that the world through him might be saved" (Jno. 3:17); "God was in Christ reconciling the world unto himself" (II Cor. 5:19); "He is the propitiation for our sins: and not for ours only, but also for the sins of the whole world" (I Jno. 2:2); "Behold the Lamb of God, which taketh away the sin of the world" (Jno. 1:29).

The texts just quoted, and many others like them, make clear the fact that the redemption of the whole world was God's great purpose from the beginning. "He made of one blood all nations of men . . . that they should seek the Lord, if haply they might feel after him and find him" (Acts 17:26, 27). Nay, more, He came Himself, in the person of His Son, "to seek and save that which was lost." The Gospel was intended for, and is adapted to, every race and clime and condition of mankind. The enterprise known as world-wide missions, then, is simply the carrying into effect of the divine purpose and project from the foundation of the world. Its accomplishment is the one sublime event toward which the whole creation moves forward, and which will constitute the consummation and crown of all God's dealings with the human race.

If all this be true, we should expect to find much about it in the Holy Scriptures, and this is precisely the case. Throughout the Bible God's thought and plan for the world's evangelization are everywhere in evidence. From cover to cover the Bible is a missionary book, so much so that, as someone has expressed it, one cannot cut out its missionary significance without completely destroying the book. For, let it be understood, Scriptural authority for world-wide missions rests not merely upon a group of proof texts, but upon the entire design and spirit of the Bible as it reveals God in His relation to men and nations, and as it traces the unfolding of His purposes down through the ages.

One writer aptly sets forth the essential missionary character of the Bible by describing it as the story of God's search for man, in contrast with all other sacred books, which are the story of man's search for God. Then follow these words: "This divine search of the Creator for His child begins with the first chapter of Genesis, and does not end until the closing words of the Revelation. God Himself is thus seen as the first and greatest Missionary, and the whole Bible as the revelation of His successive outreaches into the soul of man."

Let us then proceed to sketch God's missionary purpose and plan as these are unmistakably to be seen (1) in germ in the Old Testament, and (2) fully revealed in the New Testament.

THE MISSIONARY IDEA IN THE OLD TESTAMENT

While Christian missions in the full meaning of the term began only with the New Testament, the fact should not be overlooked that the missionary idea is to be found all through the Old Testament.

In His very first dealings with Adam and Eve as the progenitors of the human race, God revealed His world-wide design. He said to them, "Be fruitful, and multiply, and replenish the earth" (Gen. 1:28). To Noah, when the race was given a fresh start, identically the same charge was repeated (Gen. 9:1). *Diffusion* unto the ends of the earth was God's thought. Yet, strangely enough, the history of men, God's creatures, has ever since been one long and persistent effort, whether ignorantly or willfully, to evade or thwart the divine purpose which is so clearly set forth.

This fact is strikingly illustrated in the account of the tower of Babel, as given in the eleventh chapter of Genesis. Here we find a people not aiming to reach the ends of the earth, but saying one to another, "Go to, let us build us a city and a tower, whose top may reach unto heaven; and let us make us a name, lest we be scattered abroad upon the face of the whole earth." Observe here that the very thing God desired done was the thing they set to work explicitly to defeat. It was God's design, even although not yet clearly revealed, to make the human race and its redemption the means of glorifying His Son, that His name should be exalted above every name, "that at the name of Jesus every knee should bow" (Phil. 2:9–11). But *they* said, "Let us make *us* a name." Here was revealed thus early that spirit of self-love and self-seeking which has ever since dominated men and nations, and which has opposed and hindered the working out of His missionary purpose and the bringing in of the universal dominion and glory of Christ. God had to interpose, confound their language, and upset their ambitious plans. "So the Lord scattered them abroad from thence upon the face of the whole earth; and they left off to build the city."

Next, we see God choosing a man, a family, a nation— Abraham and his Jewish descendants. But with what purpose? Was it to lavish upon them an exclusive and selfish affection, regardless of all others? No, but rather that they should be His channel of blessing to the whole world: "In thee shall all the families of the earth be blessed" (Gen. 12:3). This promise, with its revealed purpose of election, was later repeated twice to Abraham (Gen. 18:18; 22:17, 18), and reasserted to Isaac (Gen. 26:2–4) and to Jacob (Gen. 28:12–14).

The same intimation is to be seen in the divine message through Moses to Israel at Sinai: "Now therefore, if ye will obey my voice indeed, and keep my covenant, then ye shall be a peculiar treasure unto me above all people: for all the earth is mine: And ye shall be unto me a kingdom of priests, and an holy nation" (Ex. 19:5, 6).

Professor W. O. Carver, commenting upon these words, says: "They must not forget that all the earth is His and all its people. If He takes this one tribe to His heart for the time it is not to forget the rest, but to do good to all. His aim is that Israel shall serve Him as a kingdom of priests, a nation set apart to prophetic service. But when the priest and the prophet are a nation, the people for whom they minister and to whom they prophesy are the other nations."

But, alas, the Jews stumbled at the divine purpose, failed to discern the meaning of God's election of them as His servant nation, and selfishly monopolized what was designed for the good of all humanity. Consequently, God had to lay that nation aside for the time as a failure. The whole story constitutes one of the great tragedies of history.

As for Abraham himself, he stands out as one of a number of Old Testament characters who were striking examples of missionary spirit and effort. In him began a long procession of missionaries which has now covered 4,000 years. His divine call (Gen. 12:1) furnishes a worthy model for that of any modern missionary, while his heroic rescue of the victims of King Chedorlaomer's raid (Gen. 14:1–16) and his importunate pleading for sinful Sodom (Gen. 18:22–33) are fine instances of missionary zeal, courage and devotion.

Joseph, too, was a great missionary, sent by God down to heathen Egypt, and used of Him for the physical salvation of the millions of that nation and the adjoining countries.

In Moses we see a true missionary leader, trained and disciplined by God for a great and difficult undertaking which called for his renouncing wealth, social position and worldly pleasure, and giving himself in unselfish abandon to the service of those who sorely tried his spirit and spurned his devotion. Like the other Old Testament prophets and leaders, he saw only dimly what the New Testament clearly reveals of the fullness of God's grace to all mankind; and yet something of the extent of the divine purpose was made known to him by God in the words: "As truly as I live, all the earth shall be filled with the glory of the Lord" (Num. 14:21).

Here and there throughout the historical books of the Old Testament we catch glimpses of the world-wide reach of God's purposes of grace. Examples of His beneficence toward those outside the Jewish fold are furnished by the incidents connected with the prophets Elijah and Elisha with which Jesus rebuked the pride of His fellow townsfolk of Nazareth (Lk. 4:25–27). A Gentile widow of Zarephath is chosen by God to house and feed His servant Elijah in a time of famine (I Ki. 17:9), while Naaman the Syrian, of Damascus, is mercifully healed of his leprosy through the ingenuous testimony of a captive Jewish maid and the ministry of Elisha (II Ki. 5).

Beautifully suggestive also of the breadth of God's sovereign love is the inclusion of Rahab of Jericho and Ruth the Moabitess, both Gentile women outside the covenant, in the ancestral line of the Messiah King. The same spirit breathes in the prayer with which Solomon dedicated the temple, when he made request in behalf of "a stranger that is not of thy people Israel, when he shall come out of a far country for thy name's sake . . . Hear thou in heaven, thy dwelling place, and do according to all that the stranger calleth to thee for; for all peoples of the earth shall know thy name to fear thee" (I Ki. 8:41, 43). The divine response was: "I have heard thy prayer and thy supplication that thou hast made before me" (I Ki. 9:3).

The book of Esther is a fascinating missionary narrative.

It presents a young woman by nature identified with a captive and condemned race, but by a gracious providence elevated to royal position and privilege. Her attention is called to the imminent peril and inevitable doom of her nation unless speedy succor is forthcoming. But the only human possibility of help plainly lies with herself and involves tremendous risk. A momentous question confronts her. Will she have regard to her own safety, comfort and advantage, and shut her eyes to the need of others? Or will compassionate concern for helpless and doomed humanity conquer all selfish considerations and impel her to attempt a rescue? As she seriously faces these alternatives, not perhaps without a struggle, right decision comes, and with it the strength and courage needed. She flings herself into the breach, regardless of all cost and danger to herself, and by her heroic action saves a whole nation. It is a thrilling missionary romance, the application of which to Christians today, and particularly to talented and privileged Christian youth, is so obvious as to need no words to enforce it.

Passing on to the Psalms, we find them pervaded by the missionary spirit and outlook. Throughout this ancient book of praise there is a constant anticipation of a King who is to reign in righteousness, and whose dominion is to extend to the very ends of the earth. Among the Psalms which are peculiarly marked by a world-wide vision are the 2d, 22d, 47th, 50th, 67th, 72d, and 96th. Take for example Psalm 2:8—"Ask of me, and I shall give thee the heathen for thine inheritance, and the uttermost parts of the earth for thy possession." Or note Psalm 67, the first verse of which reads: "God be merciful unto us, and bless us; and cause his face to shine upon us." How selfish that prayer would be if it stopped there! But it does not stop there, but goes on to reveal the missionary motive of such prayer and the result of its being answered—"that thy way may be known upon earth, thy saving health among all nations" (v. 2). And its last verse is a beautiful prophecy —"God shall bless us; and all the ends of the earth shall fear him."

Then there is Psalm 72, with its glowing prophetic picture of Christ's glorious coming kingdom, of which Solomon's was a type—"He shall have dominion also from sea to sea, and from the river unto the ends of the earth." "All nations shall call him blessed . . . And blessed be his glorious name forever: and let the whole earth be filled with His glory" (vs. 8, 17, 19).

But perhaps the richest missionary teachings of the Old Testament are to be found in the prophets, where a world-wide outlook is always clearly recognizable, even when the central message relates to Israel. The following are only a few among many passages which might be cited:

"There is no God else beside me; a just God and a Saviour; there is none beside me. Look unto me and be ye saved, all the ends of the earth: for I am God, and there is none else" (Isa. 45:21, 22). "I will also give thee for a light to the Gentiles, that thou mayest be my salvation unto the end of the earth" (Isa. 49:6). "The Lord hath made bare His holy arm in the eyes of all the nations; and all the ends of the earth shall see the salvation of our God" (Isa. 52:10). "For mine house shall be called an house of prayer for all people" (Isa. 56:7). "At that time they shall call Jerusalem the throne of the Lord; and all the nations shall be gathered unto it, to the name of the Lord, to Jerusalem" (Jer. 3:17). "For the earth shall be filled with the knowledge of the glory of the Lord, as the waters cover the sea" (Hab. 2:14). "And I will shake all nations, and the desire of all nations shall come" (Hag. 2:7). "And he shall speak peace unto the heathen: and his dominion shall be from sea even to sea, and from the river even to the ends of the earth" (Zech. 9:10). "For from the rising of the sun even unto the going down of the same my name shall be great among the Gentiles; and in every place incense shall be offered unto my name, and a pure offering: for my name shall be great among the heathen, saith the Lord of hosts" (Mal. 1:11).

Two of the prophets, Jonah and Daniel, stand out as being themselves missionaries. The prophecy of Jonah is a foreign missionary book, designed to show that God is the God of the Gentiles as well as of the Jews. It was written as a reproof to Israel in the picture it presents of a great heathen city heeding God's call to repentance in contrast to Israel, favored and blessed of God above other nations, turning a deaf ear and hardening its heart against Him. The story is also a fine illustration of God's tender concern for the heathen and His patience in dealing with them. Incidentally it furnishes an instance of a runaway missionary, whose bad example, it is to be feared, has been followed by all too many in modern times. And yet it is to be noted that Jonah finally came in line and became an obedient and successful missionary.

Daniel was another great foreign missionary whose divinely given commission, like that of the apostle Paul, took him before kings and rulers. He witnessed for God in the courts of four successive heathen monarchs, and so effectively as to lead them to recognize and proclaim his God to be the most high God, whose kingdom was universal and everlasting. He and his fellow Jews of the Captivity and the later Dispersion were theistic missionaries among the peoples of the East, as well as of southern Europe and northern Africa, right down to the time of Christ.

We have thus traced in outline the missionary idea through the pages of the Old Testament, and have seen in every part

—in the books of Moses, the historical books, the Psalms and the prophets—God's great missionary purpose and the universality of the Gospel and the final kingdom of His Son. "The whole Old Testament lives in a missionary atmosphere, and is vivified with the love of the God of the whole earth for all His children."

THE MISSIONARY HEART OF THE NEW TESTAMENT

The missionary idea which we have seen in the bud in the Old Testament Scriptures bursts into full bloom the moment we cross the threshold of the New Testament. The New Testament is uniquely and preëminently missionary—the greatest missionary volume ever produced. Every section of it was written by a missionary, with the primary object of meeting a missionary need and promoting missionary work.

To use the words of Professor W. O. Carver: "If there had been no Commission, or no obedience to its spirit, there would have been no need for the New Testament writings and no occasion for their production. A product of missions, the New Testament can be truly interpreted only in the light of the missionary idea." As another writer puts it: "The New Testament draws its breath in missions, it incarnates missions, wherever it goes it creates missions."

In considering briefly the missionary significance and teaching of the various books of the New Testament, let us begin with the Gospels. These obviously furnish the missionary with his message. They set forth Jesus as the Christ, the Son of God, the Saviour of the world. Particularly do they record and emphasize the death and resurrection of Christ as being the ground of redemption. Paul, the great apostle to the Gentiles, states this clearly in I Corinthians 15:1-4: "I declare unto you the gospel which I preached unto you, which also ye have received, and wherein ye stand; by which also ye are saved, . . . how that Christ died for our sins according to the scriptures; and that he was buried, and that he rose again the third day according to the scriptures." How vitally important it is, in these days of shifting emphases and loose ideas, to keep in mind what the real and only message for every true Christian missionary is!

When were the Gospels written, and why? They were written when the extent of Gospel witnessing became so wide that mere oral testimony was no longer adequate. Their object was to record and preserve the true message and make it available to reading men, and this work was done by four evangelists chosen and inspired by God from among those "which from the beginning were eye witnesses, and ministers of the word" (Lk. 1:1, 2).

The four Gospels, then, are missionary documents or tracts, being part of the inspired Scriptures and forerunners of the vast volume of Gospel literature which has played such a vital and indispensable part in the work of missions through all the ensuing centuries down to the present day. Moreover, the very name they bear indicates their missionary nature. The word "Gospel" means "good news." But news can be news only to those who have not already heard it, and news can be good news only to those who hear it in time to secure its benefit. Is the news of pardon sent to a condemned prisoner "good news" to him if through the dilatoriness of the messenger entrusted with the message it reaches the prison some hours after he has been executed? It is clear, then, that the very name "Gospel," which means "good news," spells world-wide missions, and that it lays upon every one who has heard the good news the solemn responsibility of taking or sending it quickly to all for whom it was intended but who have not yet heard it. The very essence of good tidings is that they be proclaimed. The first impulse in every healthy mind, upon hearing a good thing, is to pass it on to others. That is how the Christian message spread in the beginning. Andrew ran to break the news to his own brother, and Philip hastened to tell it to Nathanael (John 1). Peter and John met the Sanhedrin's prohibition of their further preaching with the answer: "We cannot but speak the things which we have seen and heard" (Acts 4:20). Have Christians today forgotten that they have been "put in trust with the gospel" (I Thess. 2:4)? Have they lost what is of the very essence of true Christian faith and discipleship?

Reverting to the content of the Gospels, we find that they give us the life story of Jesus, God's great world Missionary. The angels heralded the news of His birth as "good tidings of great joy, which shall be to all people," and the aged Simeon hailed Him as "a light to lighten the Gentiles, and the glory of thy people Israel." Both the teachings and the personal ministry of Jesus were preëminently missionary in character. Listen to His words: "God so loved the world"—"The field is the world"—"I am the light of the world"—"I if I be lifted up will draw all men unto me"—"Other sheep I have, which are not of this fold: them also I must bring."

While, as to His personal ministry, Jesus was sent "unto the lost sheep of the house of Israel," yet the whole world was ever in His vision. His thoughts and aims were not parochial, nor even national, but universal. To the woman of Samaria He announced Himself as both the Messiah of the Jews and the Saviour of the world. Of the Roman centurion He said: "I have not found so great faith, no, not in Israel," and then added: "Many shall come from the east and the west, and shall sit down with Abraham, and Isaac, and Jacob, in the kingdom of heaven." As mentioned earlier in this chapter, He reminded His own bigoted people in Nazareth of God's choice of a Gentile widow to feed His prophet Elijah, and of His healing grace extended to Naaman the Syrian. His miracles and parables alike give evidence of the breadth of His sympathy and mission. He made not only the Jews the beneficiaries of His healing power and spiritual mercy, but also the Roman centurion, the Syrophoenician woman, the Samaritan and the publican. His miraculous feeding of the multitude was itself a striking missionary parable, as a later chapter will unfold.

Finally, the Gospels culminate in the Great Commission as the real center of the New Testament, to which everything before leads up, and from which everything after leads on. Contrast the earlier restricted commissions to the Twelve and the Seventy with the new commission, "Go evangelize all nations"—"Preach the gospel to every creature"—"Ye shall be my witnesses unto the uttermost part of the earth."

In the words of a distinguished advocate of missions: "Nothing is more deeply imbedded in Christianity than its universality. . . . The Great Commission contemplates the evangelization of the whole wide world. Nothing short of this answers to the sublime conceptions and aims of its Author."

Following the Gospels comes The Acts of the Apostles, which book is an inspired record of the missionary work of the Church during the first generation of its existence. And inasmuch as the presence, authority, and mighty working of the Holy Spirit are wonderfully manifest throughout the record, we believe The Acts was designed by God as a guide and model for all later generations. With due appreciation of the value of certain textbooks on missionary principles and practice, based upon the long and varied experience of past or present missionaries, it is yet our conviction that in The Acts

God has furnished His Church with the handbook *par ex-
cellence* on this subject for all time. The thoughtful and
prayerful missionary of today will find here a divinely given
sample or precedent for every type of experience and problem he is called upon to face. Accordingly one writer speaks
of The Acts as "the authorized Missionary Manual of the
Church."

The very name of the book is in keeping with this thought.
The word "apostle" (from the Greek *apostello*—"I send")
is a synonym for "missionary" (from the Latin *mitto*—"I
send"). An apostle, or missionary, is a "sent-one," and so the
book might just as accurately have been called "The Doings
of the Missionaries." And is it not worth reflecting upon that
the Lord in naming His appointed workers thereby defined
their commission? They were not sent as theologians, or ec-
clesiastics, or philosophers, but as *missionaries* ("sent-ones"),
messengers, witnesses of His, to declare what they had seen
and heard and experienced, to make known the redemption
He had wrought for them and for the whole world. This is
still the true function and primary duty of every missionary,
however unpopular the conception may be to some individuals
today. Those first apostles, or missionaries, so conceived it, for
we read of them that "daily in the temple, and in every house,
they ceased not to teach and preach Jesus Christ" (Acts 5:42).
Their enemies unwittingly paid them a high tribute in shout-
ing angrily: "Ye have filled Jerusalem with your doctrine"
(Acts 5:28), and in stigmatizing a later group of them as
"these that have turned the world upside down" (Acts 17:6).
These leaders of the early church were, indeed, the very incarnation of the missionary passion.

Acts 1:8 furnishes the keynote for the whole book: "Ye
shall receive power, when the Holy Spirit is come upon you:

and ye shall be my witnesses both in Jerusalem, and in all Judea and Samaria, and unto the uttermost part of the earth." This verse is the contents page, as it were, of the book, stating in brief what is to follow in detail. First thereafter, in chapter 2, is recorded the descent of the Spirit at Pentecost, and His enduement of the waiting disciples with power from on high. His coming marked the natal day of the Christian Church and the inauguration of its missionary enterprise. Then follows the carrying out of the program as outlined in the key verse. Chapters two to seven are devoted to the disciples' witnessing *"in Jerusalem."* Then in chapters eight to twelve the witnessing extends afield *"in all Judea, and in Samaria,"* and we are given glimpses of Peter's ministry in the former and Philip's in the latter. In both cases the effects reach out beyond the field of initial action, as is always true of witness bearing for Christ, and so we have the stories of the conversion of the Ethiopian eunuch and Cornelius of Caesarea, as well as the founding of the church at Antioch.

Meanwhile the enemy and persecutor of the church, Saul of Tarsus, is wonderfully converted and commissioned by Christ in the glory as the apostle to the Gentiles, and the narrative leads on and out from the restricted mission field of Jerusalem, Judea and Samaria to wider and ever wider areas. With chapter thirteen begins what is generally termed the foreign missionary enterprise, and the sphere of Gospel witnessing is seen expanding (chapters 13–28) in an ever broadening outreach *"unto the uttermost part of the earth."* Peter, James, John, Stephen, and Philip are the outstanding missionaries in the earlier stages, but beginning with chapter thirteen these give place in the record to Paul as the great leader, together with Barnabas and other fellow workers.

The Acts does not close as other books do, with a com-

pleted story. It simply breaks off abruptly with the picture
of Paul at Rome, the great imperial metropolis of the world
of that day, "preaching the kingdom of God, and teaching
those things which concern the Lord Jesus Christ, with all
confidence, no man forbidding him." This conclusion is altogether fitting, for the work was not finished but "the doings
of the missionaries" were still to continue, and will yet continue until the end of the present age.

After The Acts come the Epistles. And what are they?
They were originally letters written by leading missionaries
to local mission churches which they had founded, and to a
few individual converts, in lieu of personal visits. They deal
with matters of doctrine, admonition and discipline, and with
practical questions confronting those churches, which had
recently emerged from Judaism and paganism. The three so-
called Pastoral Epistles—first and second Timothy and Titus
—were letters of instruction, encouragement and caution from
Paul, the great missionary leader and statesman, to his junior
colleagues who had been placed in positions of great responsibility at Ephesus and Crete respectively.

A closer study of the Epistles severally would reveal distinctive and impressive missionary characteristics in each. For
example, the Epistle to the Hebrews is a forceful missionary
apologetic designed to meet the hindering contentions of
Judaism, and is wonderfully adapted for use by missionaries
in every field and day, unfolding as it does the true method of
approaching and dealing with any religion which must be
supplanted by Christianity. But space will not permit of de-
tailed consideration here of the various Epistles. Suffice it to
add this word, that while in the providence of God these New
Testament Epistles have come down to us as part of the
permanent canon of inspired Scripture, their true meaning can

be fully apprehended only as they are read and interpreted in the light of their original character as missionary letters or documents.

Finally we reach the closing book of the New Testament, the sublime apocalyptic vision called The Revelation. It was written by a missionary in exile. Banished for his Christian faith to the lonely isle of Patmos, John wrote to comfort and encourage the Christians of his day who were suffering persecution under a cruel Roman emperor and a pagan government bent upon destroying the fruitful results of the Church's early missionary effort. But the message reaches out prophetically far beyond the generation to which it was primarily addressed, and envisages the final consummation of God's eternal missionary purpose in the overthrow of all worldly rule and authority in opposition to Christ, and the bringing in of His supreme and universal kingdom. The shout of exultant triumph is heard: "The kingdoms of this world are become the kingdoms of our Lord and of his Christ; and he shall reign for ever and ever" (Rev. 11:15).

Thus does the New Testament reveal itself to be in even greater measure than the Old Testament a missionary book. In its authorship and message, in its whole aim and spirit, in its very warp and woof, whether viewed in its entirety or in its component parts, it is essentially and emphatically missionary.

Having thus traced the missionary idea throughout the entire Bible, and having seen the central and vital place that the world's evangelization holds in the mind and purpose of God, it remains briefly to point out the clear and weighty implications that these facts carry with them. If the missionary enterprise is of God, if the preaching of the Gospel to the whole world is His great design and the Church's supreme business, then it follows that for any Christian individual or group to be opposed to missions, or even to be indifferent to missions, is for such individual or group to be out of harmony with God. We dare to go even further and affirm, even at the risk of shocking someone who has always prided himself in his sound Christian orthodoxy, that to be nonmissionary is to be unorthodox, since to accept the New Testament as our only and all-sufficient rule of faith and practice is to be committed, in obedience to its plain commands and pervading spirit, to world-wide missions.

Can we fail to realize that every church of today is the product of the missionary work of yesterday? Can we ever forget that our forbears were rude, degraded savages when the Gospel entered Europe from Asia through the apostle Paul's obedient response to the Macedonian vision and call, and that wherein we are different today from what they then were is all the happy result of the Gospel brought by faithful missionaries? Moreover, every Christian home, every school of learning, every hospital, every institution and law which makes for the material and moral welfare of the community and nation of which we form a part, can truthfully be said to be a fruit of this divine enterprise of missions.

What a debt do we owe to missions? Nay, what do we *not* owe to missions? Then let us think God's thoughts after Him; let us prove that we have really been made partakers of the divine nature by sharing our heavenly Father's all-embracing love and compassion for men; and let us be New Testament Christians indeed by becoming, like them, the incarnation of the missionary passion, and giving ourselves as channels for the outflow of God's grace to the whole world.

II

THE CHURCH AND MISSIONS

World-Evangelization the Church's Supreme Aim and Task

THE book of Acts contains the inspired record of the founding of the Christian Church and the beginnings of its life and ministry under the leadership of the Holy Spirit. The early verses of the first chapter give us a glimpse of the contacts and conferences of Christ with His chosen apostles during that memorable forty-day period between His resurrection and His ascension. This was His last opportunity of meeting with them, and of instructing and preparing them for the human leadership of the Church which He was founding. Surely, at such a time as this, He would choose to emphasize the things most central and most vital to this new and sacred institution which was to bear His name and represent Him on earth.

Of what, then, did He speak to them? Some answer to this question is furnished in two verses of the passage. In verse two we are told that He through the Holy Spirit gave "commandments unto the apostles whom he had chosen," and in verse three that He spoke to them "of the things pertaining to the kingdom of God." But both of these are only very general statements, and they leave us with a keen desire to know, if we may, what things in particular He discussed with them.

When we examine carefully the full inspired record as furnished by the closing chapters of the four Gospels and this first chapter of The Acts, we are impressed by discovering that only one specific thing is mentioned; and this impression becomes deeper when we find that this one and only

31

thing mentioned is recorded not merely once but actually five times. And this one thing is what? It is the Great Missionary Commission. In Matthew it reads: "All power is given unto me in heaven and in earth. Go ye therefore, and disciple all nations . . . And, lo, I am with you alway, even unto the end of the age" (Matt. 28:18-20). In Mark: "Go ye into all the world, and preach the gospel to every creature" (Mk. 16:15). In Luke: "That repentance and remission of sins should be preached in his name among all nations" (Lk. 24:47). In John: "As my Father hath sent me, even so send I you" (Jno. 20:21).

When we come to the first chapter of The Acts we find the disciples engaged in what today would be styled a dispensational discussion. Jesus appears, and they put to Him the question: "Lord, wilt thou at this time restore again the kingdom to Israel?" But He brushes aside such speculation as this, regarding it as being for the time irrelevant, and presses upon them the all-important thing of the moment: "It is not for you to know times or seasons, which the Father hath set within his own authority. But ye shall receive power, when the Holy Spirit is come upon you: and ye shall be my witnesses both in Jerusalem, and in all Judea and Samaria, and unto the uttermost part of the earth" (Acts 1:8).

Could anything be more significant than this five-fold record of the Great Commission given by the risen Christ to His followers, especially when it is coupled with the complete silence of Scripture as to any other task or responsibility enjoined by Him upon those to whom He entrusted the launching of the Christian movement? Can any thoughtful Christian fail to see that the one thing uppermost in the mind of our blessed Lord, the one great burden upon His heart during His last days and even His very latest moments upon earth, was that the message of redemption wrought out by His death and resurrection should be carried to the whole world? The very last recorded words of the ascending Christ to His disciples ere an enveloping cloud hid Him from their view were: "*Ye shall be my witnesses . . . unto the uttermost part of the earth.*"

How can we escape the most obvious conclusion that Christ founded His Church upon the Great Commission as its charter of incorporation? And it follows logically that just as every incorporated institution on earth must strictly carry out the terms of its charter or at once forfeit its right to continue, so the Church of Christ only so long as it consistently observes and fulfills the terms of its divine charter, by giving itself faithfully to its appointed task of taking the Gospel to the whole world, has any right to retain Christ's name or to claim the promise of His continued presence and power, upon which its very life and work depend.

How often do we hear that precious promise, "Lo, I am with you alway," quoted by Christians and appropriated for their comfort! But we must never forget that it is definitely linked with the command to go and make disciples of all nations, so that only those Christians who are acting in obedience to that command can rightly claim and enjoy its associated promise. Similarly, Christ's promised gift of the Holy Spirit's power (Acts 1:8) was not meant merely for the personal advantage of believers, but was clearly designed for the task of witnessing for Him in all the world, and therefore it truly belongs only to those who in some real way are sharing in that task.

Nothing is clearer, then, than that the missionary enterprise, as set forth in The Acts and conceived by the apostolic church, was no side issue, no secondary affair, not merely one of a number of equally important, or unimportant, things; it was the primary thing, the main drive, the supreme object in view which took precedence over everything else.

It is true, of course, that the early church "continued stedfastly in the apostles' doctrine and fellowship, and in breaking of bread, and in prayers" (Acts 2:42). That is to say, the church had its gatherings for worship and fellowship, and its doctrinal preaching and teaching for the instruction and edification of its members, had its sacred ordinances of Baptism and the Lord's Supper, and all the so-called "means of grace," not to mention its material edifices and equipment. But none of these, nor yet the sum of them all, was meant to be regarded as the Church's mission, nor were they in reality so regarded. They were not in themselves an end, but only so many means contributory to an end. The Church was not designed to be a reservoir, ever receiving and retaining for itself God's spiritual blessings, but rather a conduit conveying them on and out to others everywhere. Its true mission was, and must ever continue to be, the same as its Lord's—to seek and save the lost, wherever these are to be found, whether at home or in distant lands.

Are Christians really "the light of the world," as Jesus called them? Then they are surely not meant simply to be enjoying that light, snugly shut up within the comfortable lighthouse of the Church. They are to be flashing out that light far and wide, in order that mariners in peril upon the raging sea may see it and be rescued and guided to safety.

Is the Church actually an army of Christian soldiers? Then its chief function is to fight, and not merely to maintain drill, target practice and dress parade within the barracks. It is designed to be a spiritual army of conquest, engaged in an offensive warfare on a world scale, pressing the claims of Christ and assisting Him in achieving His glorious purpose for the whole human race. We do well to keep in mind that this is still the day of the church militant; it is not the day of the church at rest.

Now the truth of all that has been said will be acknowledged, we assume, as related to the church of apostolic days pictured for us in The Acts, or to the church universal in any day or generation. It is the bringing home of such truth as this to the local church of today, with conviction to the conscience and inspiration to the heart, that is the real crux of the matter. For while some local churches have caught the world vision and are cooperating nobly in the great missionary campaign, these churches are a sadly small minority. The large majority have never come within the grip of true missionary conviction, and hence have not begun to measure up to that part in the enterprise which they could and ought to assume.

With no disposition, we trust, toward captious criticism one may venture to raise the question as to what impression concerning the chief aim and objective of the Christian Church an intelligent but uninformed non-Christian visitor to America would gather from attending the regular services and observing the normal round of activities of any one of a large number of what might be regarded as typical Protestant churches in this land. Or, to come closer home, what answer would the pastors or leading members of a good many of these churches give if frankly asked to state the real aim and objective in view? It is to be feared that in not a few instances the question would cause some embarrassment and would elicit no very satisfactory answer. Judging by fairly wide observation, many pastors and churches seem not to have given this matter much if any serious thought. They have meetings, organizations, and activities of various kinds, plenty of them, yet with no very clear or definite controlling objective. They are "carrying on"

after a fashion, in ruts well worn by long use, or with only a
sort of opportunist policy, and hence their work is desultory
in character and vague in results.

How, it may be asked, is the success of any local church to
be determined? Is its achievement to be measured by the number of members on the roll, or by the attendance upon the
services, or by the financial receipts, or by the variety of
organizations and activities? Good and right as these things
may be, no one of them, nor yet the combination of all of
them, can be regarded as a safe criterion of success. For true
success can only be the achievement of an aim, the accomplishment of a purpose. What then is the legitimate and worthy
aim or purpose of a local Christian church? A number of
answers might be given, e.g., to bring men to Christ; to build
up the members in Christian faith and experience; to serve the
community by uplifting its morals, purifying its social life, and
in others ways. No one will question that these are all true and
vital functions of every church. Nevertheless, when due recognition has been given them, it still remains that all three of
these factors, if applied merely locally, do not fulfill or exhaust
the New Testament idea of a church's mission. They are all
good, but they do not go far enough.

Any church which is in actuality what it is in name—a
Christian church—is in the very nature of the case committed
to Christ to bear loyally its full share in the task of carrying
out *His* great plan and purpose in the world. The local church
as a constituent unit of the Church universal must share its aim
and mission, even as it shares its life. It thus needs to see its vital
relation, as being a part of the whole, a member of the one
body, a unit in the combined Christian forces, to the one great
Christ-appointed work of taking the Gospel to all mankind.
Further, it needs to conceive its assignment of responsibility

as properly represented not by a tiny detached area in its local town or rural district here at home, but rather by a narrow swath girdling the entire globe. In other words, every local church should be projecting itself in some vital manner into the whole world. Only as each individual unit thus contributes its part can the Church as a whole ever carry out its world-wide commission and task.

A striking illustration of this unity of aim and effort, as between the whole and its constituent parts, is afforded by such a commercial concern as the Standard Oil Company, whose field of operation extends, like that of the Church, literally the world around. Its depots and agents are to be found in the far interior of a number of distant mission fields. But wherever they are met, whether in North America or in the remotest corner of the globe, it is at once apparent that their aim, their object is one—they exist to sell oil. Since that is the supreme objective of the central organization in America, in keeping with its charter, therefore that also is consistently the end ever kept in view by each station, big or little, near or far, the world over.

A missionary writing from Manchuria told of seeing displayed by a Standard Oil depot in that far-away country the ambitious slogan: "Get the light to every dark corner of the world." Is there not in this aim a rebuke and a challenge to the churches of Christ? For the fact confronts us that throughout Asia and Africa are to be found multitudes of towns and villages lighted with the kerosene oil of the West but which have never yet had the light of the saving Gospel of Christ.

But merely deploring the facts will serve no useful end. The important thing is to locate the difficulty with a view to its corrections. It is our firm conviction that the real difficulty lies within the churches, not in conditions on the outside. No intelligent person can doubt for a moment that the Protestant churches of North America alone have ample forces and resources to carry out Christ's Great Commission within the limits of the present generation, if only they were to give themselves seriously to the task. We have but to reflect upon the record of the early church to be convinced of this truth. All missionary leaders will, I think, agree with Dr. John R. Mott when, in speaking of the Christians of the apostolic period, he candidly says: "They did more to accomplish the world's evangelization than any succeeding generation." Then how did they do it? Did they use methods which cannot be employed today? Had they any power available to them which is not available now? Such questions as these can only be answered in the negative. The fact is that the early believers were beset by not a few decided limitations and disadvantages as compared with today. In numbers they were a paltry few; financially they were poor; their means of travel were meager and crude; and of such modern utilities as the post, the telegraph, the wireless, the amplifier, and many others, they possessed none. And yet thus heavily handicapped they totally eclipsed the church of today in missionary efficiency and achievement.

Wherein, then, lay their secret? We must look for it not in the superficial realm of the material but in the deeper realm of the spiritual. A thoughtful reading of The Acts will reveal, among other distinguishing features of the apostolic church, separation from the world, a high conception of Christian discipleship, and clear and certain convictions of truth.

The separation from the world was of no mere monkish kind, but consisted in a real detachment from the world, and as real an attachment to Christ. On the one hand, those early Christians had undergone so radical a change that the world and its attractions had been taken out of their hearts, while new interests, ambitions, and hopes had taken their place. On the other hand, the world had no longer any use for them, but accorded them ostracism and persecution. Thus, as Paul expressed it, they were crucified unto the world, and the world unto them. The early church was marked by an other-worldliness; it was like an invading army in an alien land, sustained by invisible resources.

Moreover, it was a witnessing church whose whole membership was deeply imbued with the missionary spirit. The work of spreading the Gospel was not delegated to a small corps of official workers but was shared by the entire church. When as the result of persecution in Jerusalem, following upon Stephen's martyrdom, the believers "were all scattered abroad," we read that they "went everywhere preaching [lit. 'gossiping'] the Word." Of the Thessalonian converts it is recorded that "from them sounded forth the word of God . . . in every place." As to missionary giving, the Macedonian churches in deep poverty "abounded unto the riches of their liberality." It was a time of individual effort and of general consecration to the task of proclaiming the Gospel. Every Christian conceived himself as being a missionary. Little wonder is it that under such conditions as these the work moved forward and results were what they were. Without a question, the very same results would attend the church's efforts today if only the same conditions were met. The wonderful story of the Korean church furnishes a convincing evidence of this fact.

Finally, the early church preached its beliefs, not its doubts. It proclaimed Jesus Christ as the eternal Son of God, incarnate, crucified, risen, ascended, reigning, coming again. Its message dealt with sin and its sure and awful penalty, and with man's utter need of a Saviour and of repentance and regeneration. Face to face with social, moral, and political conditions and problems which were at root no different from those of today, it knew nothing of a "social gospel," but preached, in season and out of season, and without any apology, the one and only Gospel of personal salvation. Before this Spirit-empowered preaching not only were multitudes of men and women saved, and not alone were live and self-propagating churches planted, but also idolatry crumbled, slavery became doomed, polygamy and other social evils were weakened, and the whole social and political fabric of that day was profoundly affected.

Without wishing to be censorious, can we fail to see the contrast presented by the church of today, viewed as a whole, as regards the features just mentioned? In how many cases is the difference between the church and the world scarcely discernible! Christian profession in many quarters is all too cheap and compromising, and is correspondingly powerless in its testimony. Nor can it be said truthfully that more than a small minority of professing Christians are imbued with the missionary spirit and show any deep concern to win souls at home or to send the Gospel abroad. And, alas, in all too many churches the vital redemptive message of Christ is absent, and in its place a spurious gospel of human improvement, ethical culture, and social maxims is set forth. The results are tragic indeed, but their explanation is altogether clear. In the spiritual world, as in the natural, we reap what we sow, and the desired fruit can come only from the proper root.

We quote from an impassioned address delivered some time ago by a distinguished church leader at the annual gathering of official representatives of his denomination: "Why is it that the interest in foreign missions is everywhere lagging, and that gifts are falling off? It is because Christian people are no longer gripped by a burning conviction that men everywhere are lost without Christ. The sense of urgency, of immediate danger, of a crisis in salvation has largely disappeared. Many of our preachers no longer preach as dying men to dying men. Our forefathers believed that men everywhere without Christ were in immediate danger of facing the wrath of God. Our modern world has largely lost this urgent note in salvation. We need to restore it. . . . It is this loss of a mighty conviction about salvation and of both a present and a future disaster to the souls and to modern civilization without Christ that has cut the nerve of missionary obligation and enthusiasm."

If dependence can be placed upon a census taken a few years ago showing that 60,000 Protestant churches in the USA reported not a single convert for the year, and also upon the published statement that two-thirds of all the churches and three-fourths of their total membership contribute nothing to either home or foreign missions, then surely such an utterance as the above is warranted and timely, and should be taken keenly to heart by every confessed follower of Christ.

Yet happily, over against these disappointing and depressing facts some brighter features are to be noted in the picture. All through the years there have been *some* churches which have continued true to New Testament standards of spiritual life and missionary vision and endeavor. In every day, even the darkest, God has preserved a saving remnant of loyal witnesses to His truth and faithful promoters of His program. A few instances will be cited in our next chapter. It is, moreover, a cheering fact that during the last two or three decades many individual Christians and churches have awakened to a true missionary vision and been aroused to earnest effort to carry out Christ's last and great command. Today one of the most hopeful signs is the steadily increasing number of missionary conferences that are being held by local churches and groups of churches, with a view to the calling forth of new recruits for the fields abroad, and stimulating missionary intercession and giving at the home end. Some instances of this kind could be cited which are truly remarkable in their practical results, and they clearly show that if even a moderate proportion of existing churches, not to speak of the entire number, were to catch the vision and rally wholeheartedly to the task of taking the Gospel to the whole world, the achievement of that end would be a sane and practical possibility within the limits of this present generation. What an inspiring and challenging thought this is! But only a heaven-sent and mighty spiritual revival, not any organizational scheme or promotional effort of man, can possibly bring it about. In the inspired words of the prophet, it must be "not by might, nor by power, but by my spirit, saith the Lord of hosts." Considering the momentous and eternal issues at stake, nothing should be regarded by all true members of the Church of Christ as being more vital and urgent than the giving of themselves to unceasing prayer and preparation for a fresh manifestation in mighty power of the Spirit of God.

III

THE PASTOR AND MISSIONS

The Home Pastor's Strategic Place in World-Evangelization

"THE primary work of the church is to make Jesus Christ known, and obeyed, and loved throughout the world." So runs the opening sentence of a book entitled *The Pastor and Modern Missions*, written years ago by Dr. John R. Mott, the well-known missionary leader. Then follows the statement that by far the larger part of this undertaking lies abroad and constitutes what is known as the foreign missionary enterprise. The author goes on to say that the secret of enabling the church at home to see, undertake, and carry out its world-wide mission is one of proper leadership. These observations are no less true and applicable today than when they were made a generation ago. They may well serve as a starting point for the consideration of the theme before us.

It has long been our conviction that the key to the missionary problem lies peculiarly with the home pastors, since they hold the God-given office of leadership in the church, and are charged with the instruction, inspiration, and guidance of God's people in their life and service. Their position is one of high honor and privilege, but also of solemn responsibility. There is undoubted truth in the old saying, "like pastor, like people." Christians as a rule do not go beyond their leaders, whether in knowledge, zeal, consecration, or sacrifice. But they are usually ready—at least a goodly proportion of them— to follow a leader. The pastor more than any other individual, not excepting the Mission secretary, has the opportunity of influencing missionary recruiting, praying, and giving. But that influence will be exerted, and be effective, only in the measure in which he himself has caught the missionary vision, has squarely faced the question whether he ought to be a foreign missionary, has a clear conviction of a divine call to the home pastorate, and conceives of that position as designed for the inspiring and leading forward of his flock to assume fully their rightful part in the carrying out of Christ's great missionary purpose and program.

In confirmation of the opinion just expressed, we quote a few sentences from one of the most forceful of a number of books before us on this subject, entitled *Making a Missionary Church*, by Stacy R. Warburton, whose combined experience as a foreign missionary, home pastor, and Mission executive specially qualifies him to speak:

> If the missionary work of the churches is to be fully successful the leaders of the churches must come to understand the missionary purpose of the church. . . . Missions will not take its rightful place in the program of the local churches, and the missionary efforts of the churches and denominations will not achieve their full success, until pastors and other church leaders understand the primary work of their churches to be missions, of which everything else is a part and for which it is a preparation. . . . Primarily the responsibility rests upon the pastor; his attitude, his ideals, his aims, his intellectual and spiritual horizon, his interpretation of the Gospel of Jesus and of the mission of the church, will inevitably determine the interests and activities and achievements of his church.

To look the present missionary situation squarely in the face, is it not a terrible indictment against the great body of professing Christians that, 1900 years after Christ gave to His Church the Great Commission as its marching orders, fully one-half of the people of the world today still wait to hear of the only Saviour? If we seek an explanation for this criminal failure, we get at least some clue in the statement of Mrs. H. B. Montgomery, distinguished former Baptist leader, in her book *The Preaching Value of Missions*, that "less than thirty per cent of the entire membership of Baptist churches do all the giving to missions, both home and foreign," and that "men who boldly declare that they do not believe in Christian missions are found among the trustees and deacons of the church." Nor is there any reason to believe that the case is essentially different in the other denominations. This author then goes on to say: "Is it not fair to lay these defects in our church life to our ministers, in large part? Are they not our natural leaders?"

We quote also the words of a prominent minister as given in Egbert W. Smith's *The Desire of All Nations*:

> The pastor holds the key of the situation; and I do not know of any missionary-hearted pastor whose missionary outlook is always revealing itself in his handling of his ordinary pulpit themes, and whose missionary zeal is always revealing itself in his pulpit intercession, who has not gradually drawn his people into full sympathy with his missionary aim.

Inspiring instances of the truth of this observation are not lacking. One of the most striking is that of Pastor Harms' village church in Hermansburg, Germany, composed of poor artisans and farmers. Such was the contagious missionary spirit of its leader that within forty years the church sent out 350 of its members to the mission field, and at the end of that period counted nearly 14,000 living communicants overseas.

Dr. H. C. Mabie, on a tour of Asiatic fields as Secretary of the Northern Baptist Board of Missions, met twelve missionaries who had been influenced by him for foreign service during his former pastorates.

The present writer himself was one of twelve young people in an historic church in Toronto, Canada, who were caught by the missionary fire that burned in the heart of their pastor, Dr. Samuel H. Kellogg, previously a distinguished missionary in India, and all of whom found their way to some foreign field.

The churches of Dr. A. B. Simpson of New York City and Dr. A. J. Gordon of Boston, men of blessed memory, were completely revolutionized by the missionary vision and passion of their pastors, and from them went forth literally scores of missionaries and tens upon tens of thousands of dollars for their support on the field.

Quite a number of refreshing examples could be cited of present-day churches with which we are intimately acquainted, whose missionary vision and zeal have found tangible expression in the dedication of their young people to the Lord for service in foreign lands, and in wholehearted, systematic giving and praying for their support. To single out any of these churches for special mention might seem invidious, and we refrain from doing so. But the point we desire to stress is that in every case the missionary-spirited pastor has been the greatest single factor in imparting the stimulus, initiating the program, and bringing about such gratifying results. These instances go to show how infinitely greater the results would be if only many more pastors shared the true missionary vision and conviction. As the author of *The Preaching Value of Missions* says:

> In church life, in national life, in all matters of moment, people crave strong and intelligent leadership. As a rule they are eager to follow it. . . . And since the minister is the officially appointed leader, no one else, however qualified, can assume the primacy while he is there. Should he be a leader in name only, the result is a double tragedy, a shepherdless flock and a dog-in-the-manger shepherd. . . .
>
> How common it is to hear of the peculiar circumstances that

prevent a church's doing anything worth-while for missions. And how common also to see a change of pastors in that church followed by a splendid development of missionary spirit just as if those peculiar circumstances did not exist.

From what has already been said, two practical conclusions stand out. First, the home pastor must have the right attitude toward world-wide missions; and second, he must fit himself for the task of instructing and leading his church.

As to the pastor's attitude, we quote the forceful remarks on this point of an able exponent of missions:

A pastor needs to have faced the question whether he himself ought to be a foreign missionary. . . . Many a pastor has no freedom in dealing with the cause of foreign missions, from a secret fear lest if the truth were known he ought to be a missionary himself. Some pastors secretly know that they have never done justice to the question, and therefore avoid the subject when they can. Every young man entering the ministry should fairly meet the question of his duty to go into missionary work, and settle it honestly in the sight of God. Only thus can he be as conscientious in staying at home for his work as he would be in going abroad, under the sense of a divine call. —*A Study of Christian Missions*, by W. N. Clarke.

It is important to remember that the Word of God recognizes no distinction between home and foreign missions, but that these are merely man-made terms of accommodation. "The field is the world." The task is one. The last command of Christ reads: "Go, make disciples of all nations," "preach the gospel to every creature," "be my witnesses unto the uttermost part of the earth." That Great Commission constitutes His clear and definite instructions to His Church for the entire present age. Accordingly every pastor should conceive of himself as being a Christ-appointed agent for world-evangelization, to teach, to inform, to guide, to inspire his parishioners, so that they will contribute their largest quota to the carrying

out of their Lord's will and program. The missionary conviction and passion are just as necessary to the pastor at home as
to the worker abroad.

As to the pastor's duty to instruct and lead his church, we
quote again from the work of W. N. Clarke:

> A pastor who does not look out broadly upon the great move-
> ment of Christianity in the world, and is not qualified by knowl-
> edge for the task of enlisting Christians in the present work of
> their Lord, does not truly represent Christ to his people. —*A
> Study of Christian Missions.*

This remark is doubly significant, suggesting as it does that
missionary interest and effort are to be regarded not only as
necessary to the reaching and saving of the needy souls in
lands beyond the seas, but also as no less vitally essential to the
proper spiritual development of Christians at home. Christian
life is not what it should be, but is narrow and dwarfed, if its
outreach of sympathy and service is limited to less than all
mankind. Indeed, for anyone to claim that Christ is a living
reality in his own life and yet to care nothing and do nothing
to make Him known to his fellow men is clearly a moral con-
tradiction. Someone has well said, "Christianity requires per-
petual propagation to attest its genuineness."

> The thorough education of the members of the Church as to
> Christ's world-wide program is essential to their highest develop-
> ment. There is no subject more broadening, more deepening, more
> elevating, and more inspiring than this great theme. The pastor
> does the members of his church a great injustice, therefore, if he
> fails to bring them into intelligent and sympathetic relation to the
> missionary enterprise. —*The Pastor and Modern Missions.*

Alas, how many pastors, if measured by the standard set
forth in this last quotation, have grievously failed in their duty
alike to the unevangelized abroad and to their own churches
at home! While not disposed to condone their failure, we can-

not but feel that a large share of the blame rests upon the theological seminaries and other training schools, very few of which give any adequate place to the subject of the world mission of the Church, and many of them none at all. This fact is borne out by the following two statements from highly reliable sources:

> Very few [seminaries] emphasize adequately the fundamental missionary purpose of the church. Only here and there is there one found that offers its students a comprehensive survey of the church's missionary problem. . . . Most men go from the theological seminary into the pastorate with little preparation for the great task of making their churches missionary organizations.
> —*Making a Missionary Church*.

> Hundreds of young men are going out of Christian seminaries to become leaders and shepherds of churches who are not only woefully ignorant but actually indifferent; not only indifferent but in reality unsympathetic; not only unsympathetic but actually with a sense of opposition or of hostility to missions at home or abroad.
> —*The Preaching Value of Missions*.

We sincerely hope that few if any pastors who read this treatise belong to the class described in the last quotation. But we venture to suggest to those pastors who truly recognize the vital and central place of the missionary enterprise, and their personal relation to it, a few practical ways and means whereby they may effectually discharge their responsibility and fulfill their ministry in this connection.

First, it is highly desirable that every pastor should take a full course in missions—including such subjects as History of Christian Missions, Missionary Principles and Practice, and Non-Christian Religions—in some sound seminary or Bible institute. If circumstances make this impracticable, then a systematic correspondence or reading course should be substituted. He should also avail himself of good current missionary

books and magazines, and occasional missionary conferences
of the right kind—all this with the object of sustaining his own
missionary fervor and keeping informed up to date about missions.

In the next place, every pastor should initiate and maintain
a strong and systematic missionary program in his church. To
begin with, there should be missionary sermons. These messages should be given primarily by the pastor himself. It is a
lame thing for any pastor always to fall back upon someone
else for a missionary sermon. The excuse that it is difficult to
prepare such sermons will not hold. The Bible is full of missionary truth, and any pastor who gives adequate time and
thought to its study will find a rich and attractive variety of
missionary topics. Considering the importance of the subject
of missions, and the broad scope and many different aspects of
the enterprise, a missionary message from the pulpit at least
every quarter seems most reasonable. And let us add that once
a pastor turns his attention to this theme he will find it expanding marvelously, and his missionary reading will greatly enrich his regular pulpit topics by providing him with a wealth
of telling illustrations of the achieving power of the Gospel,
and of Christian faith, devotion, courage, heroism, and the
like.

Again, there should be addresses by visiting missionaries.
These messages are very desirable from time to time, and if
they are of the right kind they cannot fail to stimulate and
strengthen missionary interest. Happily, missionary speakers
are nowadays usually available in most places.

Further, missionary prayer meetings are vitally important.
One midweek prayer meeting each month may well be devoted to missions (foreign, home, and city missions all receiving attention in turn), when letters from the field can be read,

brief testimonies or reports given, prayer requests cited, etc.—all leading up to a season of united intercession. In this connection the use of missionary maps, charts, mottoes, and free literature will be found helpful. And just here may we commend the continuous display, whether in the auditorium or in some other meeting room of the church, of a missionary map of the world. This always carries its own message. The whole Bible in the pulpit and the whole world upon the wall are an excellent combination. Another thing—and one which it might be thought could be assumed and not require mention—is prayer from the pulpit for the mission fields and missionaries. Alas, it has been our experience not a few times to attend Sunday morning service in churches of prominent standing where no mention whatever was made of missionary work or workers in the pastoral prayer. Surely this is a grave omission which of itself sadly reveals a pastor's failure to appreciate the right relation of himself and his people to this great and central business of the church. But happily the opposite is to be found in many churches, where the pastor habitually leads his congregation in earnest missionary intercession.

Mission study classes are also beneficial. Quite a number of churches have adopted the plan of holding meetings of this kind weekly during the winter months of each year. An entire evening is reserved, the first part being devoted to the systematic study of some mission textbook, or field, or biography, or special phase of missions, under capable leadership, in one or more classes as the case may be; while the last part is given to an inspirational missionary address by a well-chosen guest speaker. Through the knowledge it imparts, a program of this sort serves to lay a firm foundation for intelligent and abiding missionary interest and effort and, given the right kind of textbooks and speakers, is unquestionably of great value.

Moreover, missionary topics in Sunday School and Young People's Society are of great value. Alternative plans are the inclusion periodically of a missionary topic in the Sunday School lesson scheme and Young People's program, or devoting a few minutes each week to the telling of a gripping missionary story. Nowhere is the sowing of missionary seed of more vital import, or destined to bear richer fruit, than among the boys and girls and young people of the church. Missionary letters, photos, curios, and the like, are specially useful here, and a good children's missionary library is to be strongly recommended. "The work of helping to discover, enlist and train suitable candidates for missionary service is not only one of the most weighty responsibilities of the pastor, but is also his greatest single opportunity for multiplying his own life."

Finally, missionary giving must be stressed. As a later chapter will be devoted to this subject in general, it is here touched upon only lightly, in its relation to the local church program. There is a wealth of teaching in the Word about it which no pastor can afford to ignore or neglect, although it is to be feared that many pastors and their churches have never taken this teaching to heart. Hence there have come into being the many worldly schemes and unworthy methods of "raising" money for missions, which rob Christian giving of its true value in God's sight and its rich reflex blessing upon the giver. What a poor substitute are all these man-made methods!

Among the vital features attaching to Scriptural giving are that it should be voluntary, worshipful, systematic, proportionate, and sacrificial. All these features, among others, are impressively set forth in II Corinthians, chapters eight and nine, I Corinthians 16:2, and other Scripture passages.

It is good for every church to have a definite aim in its missionary giving, such as the support of its own missionary or more than one, or of some particular station or special object; and its ambition should be to set the goal farther out each year if possible. Many impressive instances could be cited of remarkable accomplishments on this line by individuals and churches. These successes are traceable to their consecration and faith, and to the divine grace of giving abundantly bestowed upon them.

We have thus endeavored to outline some ways and means by which a missionary-spirited pastor may lead his church to realize its high calling and fulfill its lofty mission for Christ and the world. Much more could be said if space permitted. Let it only be added that in the last analysis the pastor's missionary problem, in all its aspects, is a spiritual one. Apart from real spiritual life, any or all of the suggestions offered above will avail little. The power and efficiency of the church's missionary enterprise abroad will always be in the ratio of its spiritual life at home.

The only effective basis for missionary appeal—whether for recruits, prayer, or money—is the vital spiritual experience of those to whom the appeal comes. Hence the salvation of souls through sound Gospel preaching, and the cultivation of the spiritual life of believers, should be the most vital consideration of every pastor. Genuine love for Christ and full surrender to Him, born of a realizing experience of His saving, sanctifying grace, are bound to beget missionary zeal and endeavor. Conversely, nothing will more truly stimulate and enrich the spiritual life of any home church than its unselfish, sacrificial effort for the people of mission lands. "The light that shines farthest shines brightest nearest home." "There is that scattereth, and yet increaseth; and there is that withholdeth more than is meet, but it tendeth to poverty." No home pastor need ever fear the effect upon his church of the offering of its finest young people or the most liberal gifts of money by its members for foreign missions. Rather should he unfeignedly rejoice, regarding these things as a mark of God's special favor, and as giving sure promise of larger blessing in store.

IV

THE HOLY SPIRIT AND MISSIONS

The Divine Enduement and Leadership in Missions

VARIOUS names have been given to the book of Acts. By some it has been called *The Fifth Gospel*, following as it does the four Gospel records. By others it has been styled *The Acts of the Ascended Christ*, this name being suggested by Luke's reference in the opening verse of the book to his "former treatise of all that Jesus began both to do and teach until the day in which he was taken up," thus implying that this latter treatise is of all that He continued both to do and teach after He was taken up. Still another name given is *The Acts of the Holy Spirit*. Indeed, Dr. A. T. Pierson adopts this title for his volume on The Acts, and remarks in his Introduction that The Acts is not only closely linked with Luke's Gospel as being from the same human author, but "is a proper sequel to all the four books which precede it." And in another great book of his, *The New Acts of the Apostles*, he speaks as follows: "In a word, just what the fourfold gospel is to Christ, the Acts of the Apostles is to the Holy Spirit—the inspired account of His advent, and of the birth of the Bride of Christ; the beginning of the gospel of the Spirit's presence and power; the declaration in order of that supreme secret of all holy living and faithful service, His inward working; and finally, the unveiling of His eternal identity with, and procession from, the Godhead. Truly this book is the Acts of the Holy Spirit."

When Christ gave the Great Commission, "Go ye . . . and make disciples of all nations," He linked it with the preceding affirmation, "All power is given unto me in heaven and in earth," and the succeeding assurance, "Lo, I am with you all the days, even unto the end of the age." In this great and gracious promise He provided for the extension of His presence co-equally with the extension of the Church's missionary activities. As He had been with the disciples in Jerusalem, so would He continue to be with them as they went on and out through Judea, and Samaria, and unto the ends of the earth. How was this promise to be fulfilled? The answer is: in the person of the Holy Spirit. To His disciples Jesus had said: "It is expedient for you that I go away: for if I go not away, the Comforter will not come unto you; but if I depart, I will send him unto you." By Christ's ascension and the Holy Spirit's descent, Christ exchanged His bodily presence with His then disciples in Jerusalem for His spiritual omnipresence with His disciples everywhere. The Holy Spirit became His viceregent on earth. Just as Jesus while on earth had represented the Father, so the Holy Spirit was now to represent the Son.

It is to be noted that in every one of the five statements of the Great Commission (Matt. 28:18–20; Mk. 16:15–20; Lk. 24:46–49; Jno. 20:21, 22; Acts 1:8) some reference to the Holy Spirit, direct or implied, is made. This fact is significant. World-wide missions constitute a divine enterprise directed not merely from heaven but by the Holy Spirit in person sent down to earth for that purpose. And since He was to be the Commander-in-chief of the great Campaign, its inception must await His arrival.

We are accustomed to speak of Christ's *one* post-resurrection command—the Great Commission. In reality He gave *two*: the one—"Go ye"; the other—"Tarry ye." At first thought these may seem contradictory the one to the other. Actually they were not so, but were complementary the one to the other. And both were of the same vital import. To "go" without first "tarrying" would make the going in vain. On the other hand, to "tarry" without then "going" would make the tarrying spurious. If surprise may be expressed that those disciples should be told to tarry, in view of the current evils of the day, the pressing need for the Gospel, and the urgency of soul winning, the answer is that from the spiritual point of view all their efforts would be absolutely futile without that which the coming of the Holy Spirit was to bring to them. Thus it was quite as essential for them first to tarry as it was for them afterwards to go. In other words, Christian missions and Pentecost were inseparably related—Pentecost being the essential preparation for missions, and missions being the logical and inevitable result of Pentecost.

We shall first note briefly the account of the Holy Spirit's coming, as given in the second chapter of The Acts, before discussing the object and effect of His coming as related to the missionary enterprise. The occasion was designated as "the day of Pentecost." Luke's description of the scene is vivid and deeply impressive. The disciples, in number "about an hundred and twenty," having continued in prayer and supplication together for ten full days, "were all with one accord in one place." We read that "suddenly there came a sound from heaven as of a rushing mighty wind, and it filled all the house where they were sitting. And there appeared unto them cloven tongues like as of fire, and it sat upon each of them. *And they were all filled with the Holy Spirit.*"

To this point it is the spiritual effect of the Spirit's coming upon that initial group of believers that is mentioned. But note what immediately follows—"*and they began to speak with other tongues, as the Spirit gave them utterance.*" That is to say, they at once began "in Jerusalem" the work of witnessing the Gospel, which was the primary purpose in view in the gift of the Holy Spirit. That "day of Pentecost" was the natal day of the Christian Church, and the inauguration day of world-wide missions which constituted the Church's great God-given task. And the "other tongues" find their natural explanation in the verse which follows: "There were dwelling at Jerusalem Jews, devout men, out of every nation under heaven," so that every man heard the Gospel in his own native tongue. Very fitting—was it not?—that God so arranged that on that inauguration day the entire then known world should first hear the Gospel *representatively*, through the providential presence in Jerusalem of individuals from every land, near and far! It was, so to speak, a preliminary rehearsal in miniature of the great enterprise of world-evangelization which was launched that day. The Lord brought "all the world" representatively to His disciples at Jerusalem to hear the Gospel from their lips, preparatory to the disciples' going out from Jerusalem "into all the world" to "preach the gospel to every creature."

And now we turn our attention to the relation of the Holy Spirit to Christian missions. That relation, as set forth in The Acts, is twofold: (1) the enduement of the individual worker with spiritual power, and (2) the supreme command and direction of the entire enterprise.

THE HOLY SPIRIT'S ENDUEMENT

It was no accident or mere coincidence that Christian missions began at Pentecost. It could not have been otherwise. The Spirit was necessary as the divine spark to kindle the flame that was to produce the power, and as the vital breath to fill the sails that were to impel the Gospel ship around the world. It is impressive to observe the divine order: Christ went *up*, the Holy Spirit came *down*, the disciples went *out*.

We read that *"they were all filled with the Holy Spirit"* and immediately *"began to speak"* as Gospel witnesses. And then later the more general statement follows that *"they went everywhere preaching the word."* It was manifestly a case of cause and effect.

But what is also of vital importance to note is that the essential relation of Pentecost to missions is true not only historically but experientially as well. That is to say, not only could Christian missions not *begin* until the descent of the Spirit at Pentecost, but also the enterprise could not *continue* in any real way without the continued presence and power of the Spirit in the hearts and activities of the missionaries. The same is true today. The carrying out of the missionary commission, from the beginning and all the way through to the end, is absolutely dependent upon the maintenance of the spiritual life of those charged with the task.

Wherever—whether in an individual Christian, a local church, or the Church as a whole—spiritual life has become cold and feeble, missionary zeal and effort have as a result declined. A notable example of this fact was the Constantine period, when the purity and separation of the Church were lost, and a flood of worldly evils and compromising features was admitted. There inevitably followed the Dark Ages, when the Pentecostal missionary fire burned so low upon the altar as to be almost extinguished, and the missionary work of the several centuries which followed was reduced to the efforts of a few individuals rather than of the entire Church. On the other hand, wherever a fresh effusion of the Spirit has been experienced by an individual, or group, or the Church at large, there has invariably followed a period of quickened missionary zeal and stimulated missionary endeavor. Illustrations of this order are to be found all through Church history. It was Pietism in

Germany under Spener and Francke that aroused the Church to a deeper spiritual life and produced Count Zinzendorf and the great Moravian missionary movement. It was the mighty evangelical revival under the Wesleys that quickened the pulse of foreign missions in England. It was the faith and power emanating from the godly life of Hudson Taylor that brought into existence the China Inland Mission, which God has been pleased to use as one of the main agencies for the evangelization of China's teeming millions. It was the spiritual awakening through Dwight L. Moody's visit to Cambridge and the going forth of the famous "Cambridge Seven" to China, together with the holy influence of those early years of the Keswick Convention for the deepening of the spiritual life of believers, that led to the memorable "Forward Movement" of the great Church Missionary Society. It was the fresh vision of God and the resultant rich new experience in the hearts of Jonathan Edwards and David Brainerd that moved them to cry out, "Here am I, Lord, send me!"—and which sent them forth like flames of fire to the North American Indians. One might also cite such mighty revivals in the mission fields as took place at Ongole in southern India, Banza Manteke in the Belgian Congo, Hilo in Hawaii, and Pyeng Yang in Korea, and trace in each case the wonderful results which followed, not only in the winning of souls in the local area, but also in the spread of the Gospel farther afield in the countries concerned, and the spiritual stimulus imparted to the work in other lands.

These illustrations all unite to prove that true missionary zeal and devotion can spring only from real spiritual life, and conversely, that genuine spiritual revival invariably issues in quickened missionary concern and effort. Would we see the missionary enterprise sustained? Then let us sustain the spiritual life of the Church. Would we see field operations made more effective? Then let us cultivate more assiduously the spiritual life of the missionaries. Would we lengthen the cords of the missionary tent? We can do so safely only by strengthening proportionately its stakes. Would the missionary cause launch farther out? Then it must first go deeper down. There is no other way to gain the desired results.

We write with deep conviction as to the necessity of testing all present missionary work by New Testament standards, and "rediscovering the great root principles in which the church of the first century found the law of its service and the secret of its triumph over the powers of darkness." We cannot press too earnestly the importance of recognizing, seeking, and receiving the enduement of the Holy Spirit as transcending all intellectual and other qualifications and preparation for effective missionary service. The saintly Andrew Murray wrote such heart-searching words as these: "If there is to be any hope of our working like the Church of Pentecost, we must have a new era in our missions. There must be a real restoration of the Pentecostal life and power in the Church at home. . . . The Great Commission was given in connection with Pentecost, and its fulfillment was made entirely dependent on it. . . . The Pentecostal commission can only be carried out by a Pentecostal Church, in Pentecostal power."

Is there not a real danger of Christians fearing and shunning any experience associated with the term "Pentecost" because of the distorted teaching on that theme in certain quarters, and the regrettable excesses and extravagancies which have gathered round that word? We do well to reflect that wherever there is a counterfeit there is also the *real*, of which that counterfeit is but a cheap imitation. We have long felt less than satisfied with the complacent assumption by some good "orthodox" teachers, in combating these false or extreme views of

Pentecost, that because we are "in Pentecost"—that is to say, because the Holy Spirit descended once for all, as recorded in The Acts, to take up His abode in the Church—that is the end of the whole matter, and that no concern or exercise of soul on the part of the individual believer to become possessed of all that the coming of the Spirit at Pentecost made available is necessary, or even commendable. The same reasoning if applied to the incarnation, death, and resurrection of Christ would surely lead to most fallacious conclusions. No, any assumption of this kind is in error and is dangerous. There is a world of difference between our being "in Pentecost" and our having "Pentecost in us." There is a kind of orthodoxy abroad today that is cold, rigid, critical, controversial, and that does not make for spiritual upbuilding and enrichment, full surrender to Christ, and a passion to win the lost. It is unproductive of true spiritual fruitfulness. What is needed is an orthodoxy that is vital, energetic, glowing, an orthodoxy *set on fire by the Holy Spirit*.

We hardly think that any discerning Christian would charge the late Dr. A. J. Gordon of Boston with being either unorthodox or given to fanciful views of Pentecost. Yet in his illuminating and inspiring book entitled *The Holy Spirit and Missions* he writes: "Whenever in any period of the Church's history a little company has sprung up so surrendered to the Spirit and so filled with His presence as to furnish the pliant instruments of His will, then a new Pentecost has dawned in Christendom, and as a consequence the Great Commission has been republished; and following a fresh tarrying in Jerusalem for the endowment of power has been a fresh witnessing for Christ from Jerusalem to the uttermost parts of the earth." For similar renewals of genuine Pentecostal blessing and power in our day we may well long and pray.

THE HOLY SPIRIT'S SUPREME LEADERSHIP

The Acts unmistakably reveals the fact that the Spirit came not only for the purpose of spiritual enduement of the individual, but also to undertake the corporate work of supreme control and direction of the entire movement. The work of apostolic missions was a movement personally led by the Holy Spirit. He came as the divine Commander-in-chief of the forces and the Campaign, and was at once recognized and acknowledged as such. His coming imparted the divine character to every aspect of the enterprise. The apostles responded to His leadership and became as new men. The sudden change in them from dissension to unity, from self-seeking to self-effacement, from cowardice to courage, from weakness to power, was simply marvelous and unquestionably supernatural.

We cannot here attempt an exhaustive study of the administrative work of the Holy Spirit, but would call attention to certain instances and aspects of it as revealed in The Acts, as a basis for further study.

First, He convicts and converts sinners. Think of literally thousands in that proud, conservative city of Jerusalem, so soon after the violent ejection and ignominious crucifixion of Jesus and the dispersal for the time of His followers, openly embracing this new cult and being baptized! Nor was this merely a wave of emotionalism which soon faded away, but a deep and continuing work of divine grace and power, and one that spread near and far among Jews and Gentiles alike, and affected all social classes, wherever the message of the Saviour was proclaimed. (See Acts 2:41; 4:4, 32; 5:14; 6:2, 7; 9:31, 42; 11:21, 24; 12:24; 13:44; 14:1; 16:5; 17:4, 12; 18:8.) In respect of evangelistic results perhaps no subsequent generation's record can compare with that of the period covered by The Acts.

Second, He performs a mighty work of grace in believers. If this record of sinners convicted and converted is impressive as indicating the supernatural power of God at work, no less impressive is it to observe what insignificant and unlikely instruments the Spirit of God chose, empowered, and used to this end. Think, for example, of craven-hearted Peter, who had quailed before the pointed finger of a servant girl and miserably denied his Lord, suddenly becoming the lion-hearted apostle who dared to face the populace of Jerusalem, and even the august Sanhedrin itself, and boldly charge them with the murder of the Prince of Life (2:23; 3:15; 4:8–10). Or consider the statement that those three thousand who were swept into the fold of Christ under Peter's Spirit-inspired preaching on the day of Pentecost "continued stedfastly in the apostles' doctrine [teaching] and fellowship" (2:42). For who were those apostles but a little group of obscure, unlettered, uncultured Galilean fishermen? And how could they possibly have won the attention, commanded the respect, and held under their teaching such a great and growing company in that cosmopolitan center except by the almighty Spirit of God revealed in them and working through them? The secret comes to light in chapter four, where we find Peter and John arraigned before the Jewish rulers on trial, and so manifesting in their bearing and their speech the spirit and power of their Lord that the record reads: "Now when they saw the boldness of Peter and John, and perceived that they were unlearned and ignorant men, they marvelled; and they took knowledge of them that they had been with Jesus" (4:13). And again it is seen in chapter six in the statement concerning Stephen when he was under arrest, dragged to court, and subjected to insults and false accusations: "All that sat in the council, looking stedfastly on him, saw his face as it had been the face of an angel" (6:15).

Still another evidence of the Spirit's working was the absolutely new and unprecedented standard of monetary giving on the part of those early Christians, of whom it is stated that "no one said that ought of the things that he possessed was his own; but they had all things common," and that those who had houses or lands sold them and brought the proceeds to the apostles as donations to the cause (4:32, 34, 35). And let it be remembered that these were all Jews, with their traditional propensity for acquiring and holding on to money. Truly nothing less than the power of the Spirit could achieve such a miracle as this, and one stops to think what a revolutionary effect upon the missionary cause today even a faint approach to this standard of giving by present-day Christians would have.

Third, He disciplines the church. The instance (chapter 5) of condign punishment visited upon Ananias and Sapphira for their hypocrisy is solemn indeed, and presses home the truth of the holiness of God and the sanctity of His Church. But a point not to be overlooked is the recognition by Peter of the Holy Spirit as the true and active Leader in the Church, and of the loyal subordination of himself and the other apostles to Him. Peter does not charge the guilty couple with lying *to him*, although he was the human person with whom they were dealing, but he says: "Why hath Satan filled thine heart to lie *to the Holy Spirit?*" and "How is it that ye have agreed together to tempt *the Spirit of the Lord?*" (vs. 3, 9). To those early apostles the Holy Spirit was no mere influence, but a living, present person actively administering the affairs of the Church. The only effective church discipline, and the only true means of maintaining the purity of any local church, is such a manifest presence of the Spirit of God within it that genuine believers will be attracted, while false professors will be restrained. This was the twofold effect of the Spirit's judgment of Ananias and Sapphira, for "believers were the more added to the Lord," while "of the rest durst no man join himself to them" (5:13, 14).

Fourth, He exercises authority and sends forth workers. Of this aspect of the Holy Spirit's ministry several specific instances are recorded. There is first the case of Philip (8:26, 29, 39), whom the Spirit calls to leave Samaria in the midst of an evangelistic campaign and go down to the desert to contact one lone individual, but that one a representative of the Dark Continent which had as yet had no Gospel witness. This strategy was not human but divine! Then he was further prompted as to the details of his task, and finally was "caught away" by the Spirit when it was completed. There follows in chapter ten the case of Peter, definitely ordered by the Spirit to Caesarea on a mission perplexing to himself and contrary to his Jewish prejudices, but in line with the divine missionary program, namely, the extension of the Gospel message to the Gentile world. Finally in chapter thirteen we have the account of what is commonly spoken of as the beginning of the Church's "foreign missionary enterprise," the work of taking the Gospel beyond Jerusalem, Judea, and Samaria "unto the uttermost part of the earth." Here again the Holy Spirit's personality and authority are strikingly in evidence, when to the devout and prayerful local church leaders at Antioch He said: "Separate me Barnabas and Saul for the work whereunto I have called them." In response these leaders, after fasting and prayer, "laid their hands on them and sent them away," and the record continues: "So they, being sent forth by the Holy Spirit, departed." Thus we have a beautiful picture of perfect harmony and cooperation between the divine and human agencies in the ordination and appointment of Christian workers. Later in the chapter we see the same Holy Spirit, who sent these missionaries forth, empowering them to witness (13:9) and sustaining them through trial and opposition (13:52).

Fifth, He presides over deliberative councils. In chapter fifteen we see the Holy Spirit presiding over the first recorded missionary conference, held in Jerusalem, and so guiding its deliberations that when the findings were written they read thus: "It seemed good to the Holy Spirit, and to us . . ." (15:28), just as the minutes of an official body today would read: "It was the mind of the chairman and members of such-and-such a meeting . . ."

We have here a model for church councils and missionary conferences in every day. What a revolution would take place in many assemblies if the sense of the Spirit's presence were thus actually felt, and everything said and done were at His prompting and under His control! Too often have deliberative sessions of church and missionary groups been marred by the intrusion of petty jealousies and bitter rivalries, or by resort to worldly diplomacy and temporizing expediency, with the result that the Holy Spirit has been grieved, His voice silenced, and His guidance withheld. The Lord has willed and provided something infinitely better than this for His people if they will but meet His conditions.

Sixth, He restrains and constrains workers. The narrative of the early part of chapter sixteen is more than impressive; it is arresting. A company of active, devoted missionaries, headed by Paul, start on a preaching tour into the province of Asia, but "were forbidden of the Holy Spirit." They try to go into Bithynia, but "the Spirit suffered them not." And then Paul is given that "Man of Macedonia" vision which guided them into the unoccupied mission field of Europe (16:6–10). A solemn lesson is here taught us concerning the utter inadequacy of human wisdom, even that of such a gifted, experienced, and consecrated missionary statesman as the apostle Paul, in the work of missions. While no explanation is given of this action of the Spirit of God, may we not regard it as a reminder of the fundamental principle in missions that all men everywhere have the same need, and therefore the same right, to hear the Gospel? The Holy Spirit forbids Paul to go a second time over ground in Asia which he had already covered once, until Europe is given its first opportunity to know of the Saviour.

Later missionary annals furnish us with other striking instances of the Spirit's similar restraint and constraint. Livingstone sought to go to China, but God suffered him not, but sent him to Africa. Carey's first thought was to go to the South Seas, but God guided him to India. Judson planned to labor in India, but was driven to Burma by forces which in themselves were inimical, but which proved to be providential. And that the Holy Spirit makes no mistakes is gloriously illustrated by the subsequent careers of these great missionary pioneers and generals.

Seventh, He exercises supreme ecclesiastical authority. This is clearly stated by the apostle Paul in his farewell address at Miletus to the elders of the church at Ephesus: "Take heed therefore unto yourselves, and to all the flock, over the which the Holy Spirit hath made you overseers . . ." (20:28). What a solemn reminder have we here of the supreme authority of Christ, in the person of the Holy Spirit, over all offices and functions pertaining to His true Church and cause on earth! And what need there is to lay emphasis on this truth in the face of the high claims and assumptions of historic episcopates, ecclesiastical establishments, and sacerdotal systems past and present!

We have but glimpsed in this chapter the relation of the Holy Spirit to missions in some of its varied aspects, but we hope enough has been said to press home the vital importance of according to Him His rightful place both as the One who alone can endue each worker and witnesser for Christ with the all-essential spiritual power for service, and also as the Administrator-in-chief of the entire missionary movement. What need there is to recognize and reverence Him as such, to surrender utterly to Him, and to seek constantly to discern His mind and to be led and energized by Him!

We hear much talk today about strategy, statesmanship, cooperation, and the like, in the realm of missions, and much stress is laid upon improved organization and equipment, and more up-to-date policies and methods. With no disposition to disparage these things, all of which have their proper place and value, we venture to express the fear that in these very emphases there lurks a subtle peril of substituting human mechanics for divine dynamics, and of attempting to prosecute the work of missions in the wisdom of man rather than the power of God.

We recall a striking example of this danger. Several years ago a cooperative scheme was launched on a gigantic scale for world-wide missionary advance. The budget, of tremendous proportions, was to be met by a *pro rata* assessment of the entire membership of all churches, supplemented by hoped-for help from "the friendly citizen of the world." A great central office was established, regional committees were formed, and mass meetings were held, but soon after getting off to a flourishing start the whole project collapsed, as if by the sheer

weight of its over-elaborate machinery. While the good inten-
tions of its promoters were unquestionable, the scheme was
simply not in line with the principles and methods of God as
revealed in His Word, and so came to nought.

We are profoundly convinced that the secret of true blessing and success in missions lies deep down beneath all considerations such as have been mentioned above, and that the
primary need of the hour is a return to New Testament first
principles and standards. Christian missions are no human undertaking, but a supernatural and divine enterprise for which
God has provided supernatural power and leadership. We
firmly believe that a larger recognition of the person and office
of the Holy Spirit, an increased disposition humbly to defer
to Him, and the devoting of more time to waiting upon God
in prayer to know His mind and be endued with His power,
and of less time to committees and conferences with their
wordy discussions and exchanges of human opinion, would issue in a mighty revitalizing of the whole missionary movement, and in resultant blessing and progress on an unprecedented scale.

Missionary leaders and workers today would do well to be
more concerned about getting *back-to-date*, in the sense of a
reversion in greater measure to the central aim and message of
the early church, to its aggressive evangelism, to its simplicity
and fervor of soul, and its spiritual power, and less concerned
about being *up-to-date* as regards organization, equipment,
novel devices, and the like. Back to New Testament missionary principles and practice, back to the full blessing and power
of Pentecost—this should be our deepest heart concern and
petition.

The key to the missionary problem is a genuine spiritual revival in the Church of Christ. This is the supreme need of the

hour, the only thing that will avail. We face a still largely un-evangelized world abroad, and an unchristian civilization at home. We face a powerless church, speaking in general, with apostasy in the pulpit and spiritual declension in the pew. We face the need of largely increased forces and resources to meet effectively the unprecedented opportunities in almost every mission field. Is it not a time when unceasing prayer should be ascending to heaven for such a fresh and mighty out-pouring of God's Spirit upon His Church as will quicken its spiritual life, revive its missionary vision and passion, call forth to the whitened harvest fields many gifted and Spirit-filled recruits, and pour afresh upon Christians at home the grace of giving and the spirit of intercession for their material and spiritual support? Thus would be released anew the omnipotence of God, before which every obstacle would give way and every opposing force become impotent, and the long delayed task of reaching the ends of the earth with the message of salvation would move firmly forward to completion.

V

THE APOSTLE PAUL AND MISSIONS

Salient Features of New Testament Missions Exemplified in Paul

APART from Jesus Christ, God's great heaven-sent missionary to the world, the greatest missionary who ever lived was unquestionably the apostle Paul. This is true from whatever standpoint he is viewed, whether the extensity of his missionary labors or the intensity of his missionary passion, whether his impact upon his own generation or the age-abiding influence of his inspired epistles. The effects of this one man's life and ministry upon the entire world, and for all time, are simply incalculable and beyond any words to express.

God chose to bestow signal honor upon Paul, and to give him a unique place in missionary history. Two-thirds of the entire book of The Acts is devoted to an account of his life and labors, and if the Pauline authorship of the Epistle to the Hebrews may be conceded, then fourteen of the twenty-seven books of the New Testament have come to us through his inspired pen. Since God has thus singled out this apostle for special prominence, we have good reason to accord him a large place in our thinking. And believing that Paul as a missionary exemplified the salient features of the Christian missionary enterprise as enjoined and set forth in the New Testament, we propose here to touch upon some of those features.

HIS MISSIONARY COMMISSION

In The Acts we are given no less than three separate accounts of Paul's commission, namely in chapters nine, twenty-two and twenty-six, all of which merit careful study. One of several respects in which Paul's commission was unique was the fact that it was identical in time with his conversion. This is certainly very unusual, as most missionaries would undoubtedly testify if asked. The bitter enemy of Jesus and the cruel persecutor of His followers even unto imprisonment and death is suddenly arrested by Christ in the glory, while actually on his way to Damascus armed with authority from the Jewish religious leaders to arrest, bind, and bring to Jerusalem for trial the disciples whom he could apprehend there. Smitten to the earth, stricken with blindness, he hears a voice from heaven saying: "Saul, Saul, why persecutest thou me?" Then in reply to his question, "Who art thou, Lord?" the answer comes: "I am Jesus whom thou persecutest: it is hard for thee to kick against the pricks." Trembling and astonished, Saul cries: "Lord, what wilt thou have me to do?" To this question the reply is given: "Arise, and go into the city, and it shall be told thee what thou must do." Thereupon Saul arises, still sightless, and is led by the hand into Damascus. There a certain disciple named Ananias is sent by the Lord to deal with him. Ananias lays his hands upon Saul, whose physical sight is forthwith restored, and he receives the Saviour, is baptized, and filled with the Holy Spirit.

This in brief is the account as given by Luke in the ninth chapter. In Paul's later rehearsal of the experience before king Agrippa, as recorded in chapter twenty-six, he states more explicitly the words spoken to him by Christ from heaven as touching his missionary commission, and to this passage we shall make further reference a little later in discussing the apostle's missionary conviction. But here let it be observed, as touching the incident itself, that what has to do with Paul's conversion is more simple and ordinary, while the unusual and unique features have to do with his commission to missionary service. As to his conversion, a humble disciple is sent to talk and pray with him, and leads him into the light, just as in many another case of conversion. But the altogether unique features of the incident, namely, the revelation of Christ in the glory and His personal message to Saul, seem to be related particularly to his divine call and commission as an apostle and witness to the Gentiles. Paul had not, like the other apostles, been a disciple of Jesus while on earth, and had not shared in the Great Commission given them before His ascension. Nor do we read that Ananias delivered to Paul at Damascus a copy of that Great Commission as already spoken to these other apostles. So vital was the part ordained by the Lord for Paul in the great enterprise of world-evangelization that the ascended Christ saw fit specially to appear unto him from the glory and give him this separate and direct commission. To this fact the apostle later refers when to the Galatians he writes: "I certify you, brethren, that the gospel which was preached of me is not after man. For I neither received it of man, neither was I taught it, but by the revelation of Jesus Christ" (Gal. 1:11, 12). And again, to the Corinthian church, in which were some who were disposed to question his apostolic standing, he writes: "Am I not an apostle? am I not free? have I not seen Jesus Christ our Lord?" (I Cor. 9:1).

Such then was the missionary call and commission of this great apostle. And what is the implication for us today? Are we to expect and experience a similar call and commission as a requisite for missionary service? As to its reality, unquestionably yes, although not as to all its attendant features. The unique aspects of Paul's commission were for him alone, and they need not be repeated, nor are they likely ever to be. Yet the spiritual counterpart is altogether possible, and to be expected and sought. It is of vital importance that every man or woman be absolutely assured of a divine call and commission before undertaking to go out to any mission field. Without this assurance they would be liable to discouragement and defeat before the difficulties and trials which are certain to be encountered. Each missionary today needs a sense of the divine call and commissioning no less clear and certain than that of Paul. And it is the privilege of every one chosen of the Lord for this service to have such. The Christ who cried from heaven in Isaiah's day, "Whom shall I send, and who will go for us?", and who appeared and spoke to Saul of Tarsus on the Damascus road, still reveals Himself and speaks to men, making known His will and plan for their lives. He no longer does this in visible form or by audible voice, but rather through His Word and by His Spirit.

In old China it was the custom for every high official before proceeding to his post of service to go to Peking and be accorded an audience with the emperor, this constituting an authoritative seal upon his appointment. Every missionary of the Cross needs to have had a personal "audience" with Christ before he proceeds to his field and task, and to have heard from his risen and ascended Lord the word spoken to Gideon of old: "Go in this thy might; have not I sent thee?" Thus commissioned and assured by the One who said: "All power is given unto me in heaven and in earth," he can face with calm and unperturbed spirit every circumstance and ordeal that may come.

It was thus with Paul, as the record of The Acts amply attests. When he encountered fierce opposition in Corinth, "then spake the Lord to Paul in the night by a vision, Be not afraid, but speak, and hold not thy peace: for I am with thee, and no man shall set on thee to hurt thee" (18:9, 10). Again, when he faced mob violence in Jerusalem, and was barely rescued by a Roman officer and secreted in the castle, "the night following the Lord stood by him, and said, Be of good cheer, Paul," assuring him of safety and continued blessing upon his ministry (23:10, 11). When later, on his voyage to Rome, all human hope for the ship had vanished, Paul was able to stand up and exhort his fellow travelers to be of good cheer, "For," said he, "there stood by me this night the angel of God, whose I am, and whom I serve, saying, Fear not, Paul; thou must be brought before Caesar: and, lo, God hath given thee all them that sail with thee" (27:20–25).

A first lesson, then, which Paul's missionary record teaches is the vital importance to every missionary, today or in any day, of an unshakable assurance of having been commissioned by the Lord Himself to the field and task to which he goes. Without this assurance he dare not go; with it he can face without fear but with courage and confidence all that is involved.

HIS MISSIONARY CONVICTION

Underlying Paul's missionary efforts was a strong conviction of his responsibility as a Christian to make known the Gospel to others to the utmost of his ability. This conviction was born of a firm belief in the eternally lost condition of all men apart from faith in Christ the Saviour. Throughout his inspired epistles he gives repeated expression to this solemn truth. Only a few among many passages need be quoted here, as being sufficiently conclusive. To the Corinthians he writes: "If our gospel be hid, it is hid to *them that are lost*" (II Cor. 4:3). Twice he refers to unbelievers as *"them that perish"* (I Cor. 1:18; II Cor. 2:15). He describes the heathen as *"enemies [of God] by wicked works"* (Col. 1:21); *"children of disobe-*

dience" (Eph. 2:2; 5:6); "*children of wrath*" (Eph. 2:3); "*without Christ, having no hope, and without God in the world*" (Eph. 2:12); "*alienated from the life of God*" (Eph. 4:17–19). In his Epistle to the Romans he deals systematically with sin as found in the different classes of mankind, brings a terrific indictment against the heathen world because of its idolatry and gross immorality in defiance of the light of nature and of conscience which God has given to all men, and pronounces a final verdict of guilt against the entire human race— all this as preparatory to introducing God's great plan of redemption through Christ, and salvation by simple faith in Him (chapters 1–3). And then in chapter ten he presents an unanswerable argument for the necessity of the preaching of the Gospel in order that men may hear, believe, and be saved (10:12–15).

It was on this basis of clear and firm persuasion as to the heathen's lost condition in sin, and of his utter need of the Gospel as the sole hope of salvation, that Paul was filled with an overwhelming sense of responsibility to make Christ known to those who had never heard of Him. This missionary conviction, as we have called it, he expresses in his epistles by various terms, such as debtor, trustee, steward, witness, ambassador, all of which words carry searching implications.

Without attempting here to dwell upon all these terms, let us take one of them as an example, namely, the term *debtor* as used by Paul in Romans 1:14. He writes: "I am *debtor* both to the Greeks, and to the Barbarians; both to the wise, and to the unwise. So, as much as in me is, I am ready to preach the gospel to you that are at Rome also." He does not say "I am a benefactor," much less "I am a hero." He does not seek to convey to the Romans the idea that in taking the Gospel to them he is conferring a great favor and showing unusual generosity of spirit. No, he simply claims to be an honest man, and thus ready to pay his debts. He says, "I *owe* you the Gospel, and therefore I am ready to do my very utmost to get it to you."

In other words, Paul viewed missions not as a charity, a benevolence, a philanthropy, but rather as an obligation to be discharged, a debt to be paid. With him the first appeal of missions was to the Christian conscience, and not merely to sentiment or the emotions. By his example as well as his teaching he laid the foundation of true missionary interest and endeavor upon the firm basis of duty, of responsibility. In one of his epistles he writes: "For if I preach the gospel, I have nothing to glory of: for necessity is laid upon me; for woe is unto me, if I preach not the gospel! For if I do this of mine own will, I have a reward: but if not of mine own will, I have a stewardship intrusted to me" (I Cor. 9:16, 17, R.V.). In other epistles he speaks of "the glorious gospel of the blessed God, which was committed to my trust," and of his having been "put in trust with the gospel" (I Tim. 1:11; I Thess. 2:4).

How radically Paul's missionary conviction differs from the popular conception of missions one frequently meets with among church people today! Some seem to think of missions as a mere hobby on the part of a few pious folk who, strangely enough, choose to "bury themselves" in a heathen land, shutting their eyes to personal advantages and good prospects at home. There is in general an appalling indifference and unconcern among professing Christians toward the missionary task. The majority appear at best to regard it as a charity, a benevolent gesture toward the less privileged people of other races, for whose spiritual welfare they bear no responsibility, so that anything done for them is just so much to their credit as being quite outside their sphere of duty.

Between Paul's view of missions as a debt and this easy-going view of the enterprise as a charity or beneficence, there is a world of practical difference. A debt is obligatory, constitutes a first claim, and demands one's utmost effort and entire resources to meet and discharge it. Charity, on the contrary, is a secondary matter to be taken much less seriously, and claiming as a rule only one's spare time and cash.

This brief consideration of Paul's missionary conviction brings us face to face with the very practical question of our own attitude toward missions, as judged not by any mere expressions of sentiment but by actual effort put forth. Was Paul a debtor, and are we less than debtors? Was responsibility laid upon him as a trustee of the Gospel, a steward of spiritual riches to be shared with others, and not similarly upon us? Was Paul alone constituted a witness, an ambassador for Christ, and were we exempted from a like commission? Surely the frank testimony and noble example of this great servant of Christ should stir all true Christians to recognize and seek to discharge their God-given responsibility in behalf of the millions who still sit in darkness and the shadow of death.

HIS MISSIONARY MESSAGE

No feature of Paul the missionary, as exemplifying the essentials of New Testament missions, is of greater importance than his message. That message was altogether distinctive: it was *the Gospel*, the "good tidings" of the world's Saviour which the angel announced on the night of the Nativity (Lk. 2:10), *the Gospel* which Jesus declared as He opened His public ministry at Nazareth (Lk. 4:18). In writing to the Corinthians Paul frankly affirmed that "Christ sent me . . . to preach *the gospel*" (I Cor. 1:17), and then proceeded to define that Gospel in the clearest and most explicit language: "I declare unto you *the gospel* which I preached unto you, which also ye have received, and wherein ye stand; by which also ye are saved . . . how that Christ died for our sins according to the scriptures; and that he was buried, and that he rose again the third day according to the scriptures" (I Cor. 15:1-4). This message—the statement of Christ's atoning death upon the Cross and of His resurrection—was the constant theme of the apostle and of the early church, as recorded in The Acts. Of this Gospel he boldly testified that he was "not ashamed," declaring it to be "the power of God unto salvation to every one that believeth" (Rom. 1:16), and he solemnly warned against "another gospel: which is not another" but a perversion of the true Gospel of Christ, and adds: "Though we, or an angel from heaven, preach any other gospel . . . let him be accursed" (Gal. 1:6-8).

Yes, Paul and his fellow missionaries of New Testament times were "dogmatic" as to their message. They proclaimed "Jesus Christ, and Him crucified," and witnessed to His glorious resurrection and His exaltation by God to be a Prince and a Saviour. They were likewise insistent in making direct and aggressive evangelism the center and heart of their missionary program. And rightly so, for in so doing they were carrying out the specific terms of Christ's Great Commission, "Go ye into all the world, and *preach the gospel* to every creature." With this message and this method they achieved results that transcended those of any succeeding generation. Moreover, all the marvelous spiritual and moral transformations of individuals, communities, and tribes which have followed ever since in the world field of missions have been the fruit of this same message, this same evangelism.

In modern missions Korea has stood out as a shining example to all fields because of the wonderful success of the work and the phenomenal growth of the Church in that land. But no one who is familiar with the facts can fail to recognize that the staunch fidelity of the missionaries in Korea to the true Gospel, and their commitment from the very beginning to a policy and program of vigorous evangelism, as conceived to be their primary business, have been the chief factors, under God, in bringing about this rich blessing and fruitage. A prominent Korean Christian leader, in addressing the National Christian Council of Korea, spoke thus: "The chief emphasis in our work should be evangelism. We rejoice that the Gospel has proven the power of God to transform, purify, and ennoble the lives of multitudes in Korea. . . . We believe that the supreme need today is for a re-emphasis upon the actual preaching of the Gospel itself, especially upon personal effort to bring the unsaved to Christ." If Korea's apostolic program had been the generally adopted one in all mission fields it is certain that results today would be infinitely greater than they are, and the world's problems would be much nearer solution.

That various missionary methods may rightly be employed to meet different situations is freely admitted, but all these methods must be tested by their evangelistic spirit and their compelling motive of winning souls for Christ and building them up in Him. We make bold to say that no missionary who fails in some real way to make known the one and only Gospel of God's saving grace and power in Christ Jesus can rightly be called a *Christian* missionary, whatever else he may be, or whatever else he may do for the material, intellectual, or social benefit of the heathen. For a professed Christian missionary to substitute a message of mere ethical teaching, human improvement, and social uplift is a farce and a tragedy, and is to fail of achieving results that are worthwhile and enduring.

In saying this we are well aware that there are those who insist that what is needed is a message of greater scope than that of simple evangelism, something that deals with political, civic, industrial, and economic problems. We are told that in these advanced days the emphasis must be shifted from the individual to the community, and that social service and the diffusion of a broad Christian spirit are more to the point than the preaching of any particular dogma. Accordingly the term "social gospel" has been coined and is much in vogue in certain quarters. We beg to raise an emphatic protest against the prefixing of "social" or any other delimiting adjective before the great word "gospel," with the idea of thereby improving upon the Scriptural term. The true Christian missionary knows only one Gospel, the one defined by the inspired apostle Paul. He fully recognizes the social, industrial, political, and all other implications of the Gospel. But it is his firm conviction that the most potent means, indeed the only means of any permanent value, of fertilizing these different areas of our corporate life—the social, industrial, political, and all the rest —and lifting them to a higher and purer level, and of making relationships, whether in the home, the factory, the neighborhood, or the nation, what they ought to be, is *the winning of individuals to a new life in Christ the Saviour.*

Faithful adherence, then, by every missionary today, to Paul's missionary message, "the Gospel," which, as he clearly stated, was "not after man" but was taught him "by the revelation of Jesus Christ" (Gal. 1:11, 12), and a return to that message by any who may have departed from it, are a vital need of the hour.

HIS MISSIONARY AMBITION

This ambition the apostle expresses thus in writing to the Romans: "Making it my aim so *to preach the gospel, not where Christ was already named*, that I might not build upon another man's foundation; but, as it is written, They shall see, to whom no tidings of him came, and they who have not heard shall understand" (Rom. 15:20, 21, R.V.).

Paul was not content simply to join the ranks of Christian workers in home fields where already so many were engaged. His was a great pioneer spirit that longed to reach out beyond the bounds of existing effort and "occupied" areas, to invade new territory with the glorious evangel, to set up the banner of the Cross on virgin soil where Christ's name had never yet been heard. *"The regions beyond"* was the motto of this splendid missionary, the slogan of this "good soldier of Christ Jesus," who never gave a thought to the cost to himself of his service, but desired only to "please him who enrolled him as a soldier." What a noble ambition! What a challenging example to others! Would that many more young Christians to-day would emulate it!

History is replete with instances of high ambition, amounting indeed to a burning passion, for military conquest and expansion of empire. We think of an Alexander, a Xerxes, a Kublai Khan, a Julius Caesar, a Napoleon, not to mention others of more recent times. There have also been those who have been consumed with an ambition for geographical exploration. How many lives have been laid down, and what fabulous sums of money expended, in expeditions to reach the North and South Poles, or to scale the heights of the Himalayas! But, however worthy or unworthy these various adventures and undertakings may have been, they all pale into insignificance before the sublime aim and goal of Christian missions—the pushing out of the frontiers of the heavenly kingdom, the proclaiming of Christ to the ends of the earth, the reaching of millions of men and women with infinite potentialities but who are hopelessly sunken in the depths of sin, degradation and misery, and lifting them through the knowledge of a Saviour into a new life of purity, joy, and eternal hope.

It is hard to understand how the soul of Christian youth is not filled with holy ambition, born of loving loyalty to Christ and strong compassion for lost and suffering multitudes, to dedicate their lives, with all their God-given talents and capabilities, to this greatest and noblest cause in all the world, that of "preaching the gospel in the regions beyond," where as yet the name of Christ has never been heard. Every "unoccupied" area and unevangelized tribe or community in the world today, nineteen hundred years after the Great Commission was given, is a sad reproach upon the fair name of Christ, and a shameful reflection upon the Church which professes allegiance to Him. God's words to Israel years after they had entered the Promised Land are truly applicable to His Church today with reference to the missionary "land of promise" (Psa. 2:8): "There remaineth yet very much land to be possessed. . . . How long are ye slack to go to possess the land which the Lord God of your fathers hath given you?" (Josh. 13:1; 18:3).

A former missionary on the borders of Tibet wrote these impressive words: "The eyes of Christians should turn as instinctively toward the lands closed to the Gospel in this missionary age as do the eyes of a conquering army toward the few remaining outposts of the enemy which withstand the victors and hinder complete victory, and without which the commander-in-chief is unable to close the campaign."

HIS MISSIONARY CAREER

The geographical area covered by the missionary labors of Paul is truly amazing, and the more so when we take into consideration the times in which he lived. A brief summary of his travels is furnished us in the fifteenth chapter of Romans, where after a humble and grateful reference to the infinite grace of God by which he was entrusted with the ministry of the Gospel among the Gentiles, he goes on to say: "I will not dare to speak of any things save those which Christ wrought through me, for the obedience of the Gentiles, by word and deed, in the power of signs and wonders, in the power of the Holy Spirit; so that *from Jerusalem, and round about even unto Illyricum, I have fully preached the gospel of Christ* . . . Wherefore also I was hindered these many times from coming to you [i.e. to Rome]: but now, having no more any place in these regions, and having these many years a longing to come unto you, *whensoever I go unto Spain* (for I hope to see you in my journey, and to be brought on my way thitherward by you . . .)—but now, I say, I go unto Jerusalem, ministering unto the saints. . . . When therefore I have accomplished this . . . *I will go on by you unto Spain*" (vs. 18–28, R.V.).

Let us try to take in, preferably with the aid of a map before us, the extent of territory included in the above statement. First of all, "*from Jerusalem, and round about even unto Illyricum*," writes Paul. His itinerary took him northward from Jerusalem through Palestine into Syria; thence north-westward over the various proconsular divisions of Asia Minor; then across the Aegean Sea into Macedonia; from there southward into Achaia (Greece); and finally to the north-west again as far as Illyricum, the region now known as Albania, lying on the eastern shore of the Adriatic Sea across from Italy. But Paul also makes mention of his hope later on to visit Rome, and to make that a stepping stone on his way to distant Spain, on the extreme western confines of Europe.

As to Rome, we well know that Paul not only reached that great metropolis, but also spent some years there as a prisoner and finally suffered death as a martyr. There is good evidence also to support the belief of careful Bible students that the apostle was released after two years' imprisonment and remained free for several years, during which time he revisited Asia Minor and Macedonia and carried out his long cherished purpose to visit Spain. Assuming this to be so, the scope of this one man's movements and achievements as a missionary is altogether unique and unequaled in missionary annals. For, let it be remembered, Paul lived centuries before the existence of any of the modern modes of travel. In his day there were no railroads, steamships, motor cars, or airplanes, and no facilities such as the telegraph, telephone, and wireless. His long land journeys were hard and fatiguing, made over poor roads upon the back of animals or on foot, while his sea voyages in crude, comfortless, slow-moving sailing craft were at the risk of his life, as the one instance recorded in The Acts illustrates.

A well known biographer of Paul, discussing one of his several missionary tours, affirms "that in its issues it far outrivaled the expedition of Alexander the Great, when he carried the arms and civilization of Greece into the heart of Asia, or that of Caesar when he landed on the shores of Britain, or even the voyage of Columbus when he discovered the new world. The whole world is different from what it would have been because of what Paul did while serving Christ as a foreign missionary. He made all nations his beneficiaries."

Among all missionaries since Paul's day, perhaps those who can be regarded as most nearly approaching him in respect of extensity of operation and magnitude of accomplishment, are Francis Xavier, impassioned Jesuit of the sixteenth century, William Carey of India, "Father of Modern Missions," David Livingstone, prince of missionary explorers and pioneers in Africa, and John Williams, "Apostle of the South Seas." But above even these great heroes towers the unique, incomparable apostle Paul.

Part of Paul's prayerful desire expressed in Philippians 3:10 was "that I may know . . . the fellowship of his [Christ's] sufferings." The abundant measure in which that longing was realized is attested by his recorded experiences. Take for example the impressive epitome given in II Corinthians chapter eleven: ". . . in labors more abundant, in stripes above measure, in prisons more frequent, in deaths oft. Of the Jews five times received I forty stripes save one. Thrice was I beaten with rods, once was I stoned, thrice I suffered shipwreck, a night and a day I have been in the deep; in journeys often, in perils of robbers, in perils by mine own countrymen, in perils by the heathen, in perils in the city, in perils in the wilderness, in perils in the sea, in perils among false brethren; in weariness and painfulness, in watchings often, in hunger and thirst, in fastings often, in cold and nakedness. Beside those things that are without, that which cometh upon me daily, the care of all the churches" (vs. 23–28).

Other passages might be quoted, such as I Corinthians 4:9–13, and II Corinthians 4:8–12, which give further insight into the suffering aspect of this apostle's missionary career, while the arresting fact speaks for itself that altogether about one-half of his entire period of service was spent in prison. Then came the climax to this long record of suffering, as he laid his head on the block, condemned by the cruel emperor Nero, and died a martyr for Jesus Christ. If all this seems to human reasoning to be wrong and unfitting, let it be noted that Paul's very call to missionary service was couched in terms of suffering. The ascended Saviour's words to Ananias concerning Saul of Tarsus were *not* "I will shew him how great things he must *attempt*, or must *achieve* . . . ," but "I will shew him how great things he must *suffer* for my name's sake" (Acts 9:16).

All this serves to correct the popular but quite erroneous idea that suffering in missionary life and labor is to be regarded as extraneous, accidental, and in the nature of a misfortune. While from the human viewpoint it may be so looked upon, the Word of God clearly reveals it to be neither accidental nor merely incidental, but actually part of the ordained program of missions from beginning to end. Jesus, God's "world missionary" and greatest of all sufferers, said to His disciples, "If they have persecuted me, they will also persecute you" (Jno. 15:20), and again, "Behold, I send you forth as sheep in the midst of wolves" (Matt. 10:16). In The Acts, that inspired record of the beginning of Christian missions and model for all subsequent generations, we find insult, violence, persecution, imprisonment, and martyrdom running through its pages from start to finish. These things were not mere exceptions to rule, but were rather the norm of apostolic missionary experience. Those early missionaries accepted them as such, nor did it seem ever to occur to them that because of their sufferings and dangers they should suspend their operations or diminish their efforts. They "rejoiced that they were counted worthy to *suffer shame for his name*" (5:41). When released from detention by the authorities with a threat of worse punishment if they did not desist, their prayer was not for vindication, not for revenge, not for exemption from further ill treatment, but simply for strength and courage to go on undaunted as good soldiers of Christ and fulfill their ministry, whatever the cost to themselves (4:29).

Paul himself on his last journey to Jerusalem, when given clear intimation that "bonds and affliction" awaited him there, responded: "None of these things move me, *neither count I my life dear unto myself*, so that I might finish my course with joy . . ." (20:24). And writing later to the Philippian church he said: "Unto you it is given in the behalf of Christ, not only to believe on him, *but also to suffer for his sake*" (Phil. 1:29).

Christian missions ever since Paul's day have been one continuous record of suffering and sacrifice. The ruins of the old Colosseum at Rome still bear silent witness to the early martyrs who were there flung to the fury of the wild beasts, as also do the catacombs to the hundreds of thousands of faithful Christians who sought refuge within them from their cruel persecutors, and later died and were buried there. If space permitted, a well-nigh interminable list could be given of later heralds of the Cross throughout the world whose obedience to the Great Commission involved for them cruel treatment and suffering of every kind, and many of whom finally sealed their testimony with their blood.

We think of Raymond Lull stoned to death by a Moslem mob, of Judson languishing in a filthy prison in Burma, of Livingstone enduring untold hardships and bitter opposition in Africa, of Mackay cruelly persecuted and Hannington foully murdered in Uganda. We recall John Williams and the other martyrs of Erromanga, James Chalmers felled to death by a savage in New Guinea, Bishop Patteson suffering a similar fate in Melanesia, Allen Gardiner also and his six brave companions perishing of starvation on the desolate shore of Tierra del Fuego. The fateful "Boxer Year" in China, with its ghastly toll of 189 Protestant missionary martyrs, is still a vivid memory. All these are but a few among the host of noble men and women who as ambassadors for Christ among the heathen have *"loved not their life unto the death."* Countless others who have not been called upon to suffer martyrdom in the literal sense have been no less valiant soldiers of Christ in holding on courageously through long years in the far-flung battle line of missions, facing hardship, opposition, danger, and trial of every kind.

What shall we say as to all this? Some may regard all these adverse experiences as just so much inevitable misfortune connected with missionary life which must be endured stoically, while there are others who would even repeat the question of one of old, "To what purpose is this waste?" But a careful examination of the actual record reveals the fact that these so-called liabilities proved in reality to be profitable assets.

Turning back first to The Acts, we have at the very outset the stoning of Stephen, the first Christian martyr. That was a blow of Satan aimed at crushing the missionary movement at its start. But instead of thus extinguishing the Gospel fire he only succeeded in spreading the embers to ignite on every hand, so that we read, "They that were scattered abroad went everywhere preaching the word" (8:4). As a result, a multitude in Jerusalem believed, and the work extended far afield. May it not be, indeed, that Stephen's martyrdom was the first step in the conversion of the great apostle Paul? This is suggested by Paul's touching reference in Acts 22:20 to that event and his connection with it. One even wonders whether Timothy, Paul's brightest convert and truest yokefellow, may not have been the fruit of the apostle's own stoning at Lystra, Timothy's home town. At all events, we do know that the conversion of the Philippian jailer and his household was the direct outcome of the flogging and imprisonment of Paul and Silas, as told in chapter sixteen. And as later on the old warrior drew near to his martyr death, he wrote from another prison to the church in that very city of Philippi which had sprung up through his sufferings, testifying that "the things which happened unto me have turned out rather unto the progress of the gospel; so that my bonds became manifest in Christ to the whole pretorium and to all the rest" (Phil. 1:12, 13, R.V.) God's way of carrying the Gospel message to the proud and wicked emperor of Rome and his entire court was by means of this missionary's sufferings which ended in martyrdom.

To cite but one further instance in The Acts of the fruit of suffering, we turn to chapter twelve, where Peter's imprisonment and narrow escape from death issued, through believing prayer, in the advancement of the work. There we read that Herod, the persecutor of the Church, "was eaten of worms, and gave up the ghost," while "the word of God grew and multiplied." Here again we see missionary suffering not merely neutralized by God, but turned to positive blessing and advantage to the cause.

Illustrations of the place of suffering in missions lie thick on the pages of all subsequent history down to the present time. Just a few can here be given, relating respectively to the South Seas, Africa, and China.

It was in 1839 that John Williams, "Apostle of the South Seas," after a wonderful career on other islands, stepped ashore upon the cannibal island of Erromanga, only to be promptly felled by the club of a brutal savage. But just fifty years later, one of the sons of that murderer was to be seen laying the foundation stone of a martyr memorial church on the island, while another son was preaching the Gospel for which the martyr died. The story of missions in Uganda is one of dark tragedy leading on to glorious triumph. The earliest missionaries met with fierce opposition, and several of them together with many of their converts were brutally murdered. Alexander Mackay, the best-known of the pioneers, died in 1890 facing the foe, having been permitted to see little fruit of his heroic efforts. But only twenty-nine years later, 2,000 churches and a Christian community of over 100,000 bore witness to the fruitfulness of those sacrificial labors. In the year 1919 the Cathedral of Kampala was built, the largest church in all Africa, and at its dedication was filled to capacity, with 20,000 on the outside unable to get in. Uganda, once called the darkest spot in Africa, had become known as the brightest spot.

Turning to China, we note the sequel to that mass murder of missionaries by the Boxers in 1900, to which reference has already been made. When, just seven years later, the Centenary Conference of Protestant Missions in China was held in Shanghai, it was found that for every missionary martyred in 1900 a thousand converts had been received into the churches, and the visible results in baptized converts for the seven years following the Boxer uprising were actually double those of the preceding ninety-three years of the century.

Perhaps no missionary incident in recent years has stirred more widespread feeling than the murder of John and Betty Stam of the China Inland Mission, who were captured and be-headed by bloody Communist insurgents in 1934. Lovely and full of promise as their lives were, their martyr death counted more for Christ and His cause in China than any prolonged service on earth could possibly have done. What the world called a tragedy, but what their biographer rightly termed a triumph, perceptibly quickened the pulse of missionary interest in North America and the other homelands, and led scores if not hundreds of young Christians to dedicate themselves to missionary service.

That oft-quoted saying about the blood of the martyrs being the seed of the Church has been proven a thousand times over to be no mere platitude, but a living, pulsating truth. Again and again God has been pleased to accomplish on the mission field through adversity, bitter opposition, and even cruel martyrdom, what seemed impossible of achievement by means of what we are wont to term the normal processes of missionary work. It is then for His servants to leave with Him the choice, concerned only to be "good soldiers of Christ Jesus," ready to glorify Him whether by life or by death, whichever His unerring love and wisdom may ordain.

HIS MISSIONARY PASSION

It has already been stated in this chapter that Paul's missionary efforts rested not upon any weak and shifting basis of sentiment but rather upon the solid ground of conscientious conviction; that he viewed missions not as a mere philanthropy in which to indulge, but as a binding obligation to be discharged. But it would be far from correct to interpret this as simply a stern, legal attitude on his part, devoid of any feeling. The appeal of missions spoke not alone to his conscience, but to his heart as well. Once convinced that he was a debtor to all men to give them the Gospel, he responded wholeheartedly with the words, "So, as much as in me is, *I am ready* to preach the gospel to you also that are at Rome." Thus missionary conviction ripened into missionary passion that filled his soul and poured itself out in sacrificial endeavor.

Listen to the impassioned words of his Roman epistle: "Brethren, my heart's desire and prayer to God for Israel is, that they might be saved" (Rom. 10:1); "I say the truth in Christ, I lie not . . . that I have great heaviness and continual sorrow in my heart. For I could wish that myself were accursed from Christ for my brethren, my kinsmen according to the flesh" (Rom. 9:1, 2). Or again, his words to the Corinthians: "The love of Christ constraineth us" (II Cor. 5:14);

"I will very gladly spend and be spent for your souls" (II Cor. 12:15).

As these expressions and others in his writings reveal, the great apostle's missionary service was actuated by a spirit of fervent love and loyalty to Christ his Lord and Saviour, and of deep compassion for the souls whom Christ died to redeem. In this, as in much else, he furnishes an example which may well be emulated by all missionaries today. There is ever the danger of becoming professional, and almost mechanical, in our Christian service, whether on the mission field or at home, and of thinking and acting in terms of some particular program or enterprise in hand, and of becoming, more or less, merely useful cogs in a machine. What need there is of a constant renewal within one's heart of compassionate love for souls, and of burning zeal to win them to the Saviour! Without this our ministry will surely fail of achieving its truest and highest end.

The following quotation is impressive as bearing upon this vital factor. It is from a message given to a class of students in training for the ministry: "The trouble with Christianity today is not so much ignorance as indifference. It has lost its passion. You will meet a high type of scholarship all about you. The preachers of today will compare in elegance and refinement most favorably with those of any day, but more than culture and eloquence is needed. All through the years it has been the passionate souls that have stirred men: men of passion like that of Moses when he cried out to God for the forgiveness of the people's sin 'and if not, blot me, I pray thee, out of thy book which thou has written'; that passion that could sing in the heart of Paul in the midnight dungeon; that passion which in the early years of Christianity fed the fires of persecution, never counting life dear unto itself. Passion prevails when intellect fails without it. . . . May your words be hissing hot from a heart on fire with a loving devotion. May you be 'Heralds of Passion!' "

"Heralds of Passion"—what an arresting word! Yet it truly fits the apostle Paul, as The Acts and the Pauline epistles abundantly reveal. And there are others of kindred spirit who come to mind. We hear Zinzendorf exclaiming, "I have one passion—it is He, and He alone." We listen to the cry of Henry Martyn, as he stepped ashore in India, "Now let me burn out for God." We sense something of Livingstone's passion of soul for dark Africa in his words, "I will open a way to the interior or perish," and Hudson Taylor's similar passion for the land of Sinim when he wrote, "I feel as if I could not live if something is not done for China." We catch the fervid spirit of David Brainerd in his journal entry, "I wanted to wear out my life in His service, for His glory . . . I cared not where or how I lived or what hardships I went through, so that I could but gain souls for Christ."

The writer has vivid memories of a great preacher of years ago who laid repeated emphasis upon the two words VISION and PASSION, as expressing two great essentials for the Christian ministry. How clearly are both of these qualities exemplified in this noble apostle with whom the present chapter has dealt! We do well to ponder them, as well as all the other features of his missionary character and career which have been passed in review, and then to heed his inspired admonition, "Be ye followers of me, even as I also am of Christ."

VI

CHRIST'S RETURN AND MISSIONS

The True Perspective and Goal of Missionary Effort

IF WE are to hope for success in any undertaking we must have at the outset clear ideas of the end in view. Even in the ordinary things of life this is obviously true. Which of us would board a train simply with a notion of "going somewhere"? No, we would have some definite place in mind and a ticket in hand for that destination. Nor would any intelligent builder set his workmen to using the materials assembled without first having drawn up specific plans for the structure in mind, and having blueprints carefully made. In other words, right thinking must always precede right acting.

If this is important in the lesser affairs of everyday life, how much more important is it as related to a divine enterprise of the gigantic proportions of world-wide missions! God is never vague or haphazard in His planning and working; He is always foreseeing and precise. "Known unto God are all his works from the beginning of the world" (Acts 15:18). The expression "by whom also he made the worlds" in Hebrews 1:2, which refers to the Son of God, would read more literally, "by whom also he constructed the ages," suggesting that the pre-existent Christ was the Great Architect not only of the material universe but also of the ages or dispensations of time, fitting them together in proper sequence for the outworking of His one preconceived, majestic, and eternal plan and purpose.

For a clear understanding of God's missionary plan and

program we naturally turn first to Christ's Great Commission as constituting the direct and authoritative divine instructions to the Church, and then to The Acts as the inspired record of the inauguration of the movement and its progress during the first thirty years.

As already mentioned in an earlier chapter, five statements of the Great Commission are given, one in each of the four Gospels, and one in The Acts. It is to be observed, moreover, that by all four of the writers of the Gospels the coming of the Lord is linked with the Great Commission, either directly or indirectly. Matthew's version of the Commission includes the promise of the presence of Christ with His missionaries "unto the consummation of the age" (28:20, R.V. Marg.). Luke links the two closely together in the first chapter of The Acts. Mark quotes Jesus' words, "And the gospel must first be published among all nations," as a part of the Olivet discourse concerning His coming. John, who alone omits the Olivet discourse (possibly in view of the fact that he was to write The Revelation), yet refers to the Lord's return by recording Jesus' words to Peter about John: "If I will that he tarry till I come, what is that to thee?"

Turning now to The Acts, we find that no statement of the task assigned by Christ to His Church could well be more unmistakably clear than that of chapter one, verse eight: "Ye shall receive power, when the Holy Spirit is come upon you: and ye shall be my witnesses both in Jerusalem, and in all Judæa and Samaria, and unto the uttermost part of the earth." These are the last recorded words of Christ on earth, for we read that "when he had said these things, as they were looking, he was taken up; and a cloud received him out of their sight." And then note what immediately follows: "And while they were looking stedfastly into heaven as he went, behold two men stood by them in white apparel; who also said, Ye men of Galilee, why stand ye looking into heaven? this Jesus, who was received up from you into heaven, shall so come in like manner as ye beheld him going into heaven" (vs. 9–11).

Here we see closely and significantly joined together two vital matters: first, the risen Lord's marching orders to the Church to take the Gospel to the whole world; and second, the announcement by heavenly messengers that He would come back, personally and visibly as they had just seen Him go. That these two things—the world-wide mission of the Church and the "blessed hope" of the Lord's return—are thus intimately related the one to the other is surely altogether obvious. The departing Lord left a distinctive program, an engrossing task, for His Church to carry out during His absence, and the promise of His return was added, the natural inference being that He would come when that program was fulfilled, that task completed. Moreover, this inference is made the stronger, and the lesson of the passage becomes the more impressive, when we note the incident recorded in the earlier verses of this chapter which led up to Christ's statement of the Great Commission in verse eight. The risen Lord comes upon His apostles engaged in what would today be termed a dispensational discussion. They ask Him, "Lord, dost thou at this time restore the kingdom to Israel?"—a very natural question for them, as Jews, to ask. But His reply is, "It is not for you to know times and seasons, which the Father hath set within his own authority. But . . ." But what? "But ye shall be my witnesses . . . unto the uttermost part of the earth."

Can anyone fail to see the point? The Lord brushes aside their discussion about "times and seasons" as irrelevant for the time being, and presses home the thing that *was* relevant, and of vital importance, namely, that they give themselves unreservedly to the one great business and prime objective of the Church for the present age, the evangelization of the entire world. Is this not a word in season to the Lord's people today, and to certain of their leaders in particular, bidding them give less attention to "times and seasons," or in other words, to profound but largely academic discussions and controversies over various fine points of prophetic interpretation, about which there have always been differences of opinion and always will be, and to devote their time and talents more to the practical aspect of the subject, the carrying out to completion of their risen Lord's last expressed wish and command?

Two mistakes might have been made by the disciples who heard the Great Commission from the lips of Jesus, as above quoted: (1) *making the task too small,* by confining their attention to Jerusalem alone, or to Judæa and Samaria at most, and thus failing to carry out to the full their orders, which read "and unto the uttermost part of the earth," or (2) *making the task too big,* by wrongly interpreting the Commission to mean that what was to be accomplished was the conversion of the whole world. In point of fact, these two errors have been sadly prevalent within the Church throughout the years that have followed, and have accounted in large measure for the failure to carry out to completion the real task enjoined by Christ.

The first of these two errors, that of limiting Gospel effort to any home land constituting only a small section of the world, must be regarded as an error of the heart rather than of the intelligence. It is that selfishness, that racial prejudice, that cold unconcern for the spiritual welfare of those beyond one's own people, neighborhood, or nation, which takes refuge behind such flimsy excuses as "there is work enough to do at home," "the heathen have their own religions," and the like.

And, just in passing, it may be noted that these arguments are usually advanced by persons who habitually do little or nothing to advance the Gospel even at home where they are. But consideration of this error does not fall within the scope of our present chapter, and so it is to the second error that we now turn our attention.

Those who regard the work committed by Christ to His Church to be the conversion of the whole world through Gospel effort—and there have been, and still are, many sincere Christians who hold this view—can find no ground for this belief in the wording of the Great Commission as given in Acts 1:8, where the command reads simply, "be my witnesses." Nor yet does any one of the other four statements of the Great Commission express or imply such a view. In Matthew the reading is, "teach [more literally, 'make disciples of'] all nations" (28:19). In Mark it is, "preach the gospel to every creature" (16:15), and the words which follow—"he that believeth and is baptized shall be saved; but he that believeth not shall be condemned"—clearly exclude the view that *all* will accept the message and be saved. In Luke the statement is, "that repentance and remission of sins should be preached in his name among all nations" (24:47). Finally, John quotes Jesus as saying, "As my Father hath sent me, even so send I you" (20:21), which words declare an identity between the mission of Jesus and that of His disciples, and this identity applies both to the message proclaimed and to its reception. As some received *His* message, while others rejected it, so would it be in *their* case.

A careful reading of these five different renderings of the Great Commission should make it clear to anyone that their language does not warrant the view that the task committed to the Church was that of converting the world. Nor can any other Scripture be cited which rightly interpreted supports this view. What Christ *did* enjoin was the proclaiming of the Gospel to the entire world, that men everywhere might have opportunity to hear and accept it, and be saved. The word *"witness,"* used in Acts 1:8 and in so many other New Testament passages, really furnishes the true keynote for the program of missions in this age. The Church was charged not with the task of winning the whole world, but of witnessing to the whole world; not with the responsibility of bringing all men to Christ, but of taking Christ to all men. In other words, the goal set for its missionary effort was not world-wide conversion, but world-wide evangelization. Between these two objectives there is obviously a vast difference.

One passage in The Acts which perhaps more than any other sets forth explicitly the New Testament program of missions is that in the fifteenth chapter which gives an account of the Church's first missionary conference at Jerusalem. The occasion of that gathering was a dispute which had arisen over the receiving of Gentiles into the Church without their undergoing the Jewish rite of circumcision. In defense of this action, Peter recited the thrilling story of how God led him to Cornelius and his company at Cæsarea, and set His seal of approval upon their acceptance and baptism by granting an effusion of the Spirit upon them. Barnabas and Paul followed, "declaring what miracles and wonders God had wrought among the Gentiles by them" on their recent missionary tour in Asia Minor.

Thereupon James, the presiding officer, spoke as follows: "Simeon [Peter] hath rehearsed how first God visited the Gentiles [nations], to take out of them a people for his name. And to this agree the words of the prophets; as it is written, After these things I will return, and I will build again the tabernacle of David, which is fallen; and I will build again the ruins thereof, and I will set it up: That the residue of men may seek after the Lord, and all the Gentiles upon whom my name is called, saith the Lord, who maketh these things known from of old" (R.V.). This passage is here quoted in full because of its direct and important bearing upon the question of the Church's part in God's great program of reaching the world with the Gospel. According to James' statement, that program, in so far as it relates to the Gentiles, consists of two stages: (1) *an elective stage*, following the rejection of Israel after Christ's first coming; and (2) *a universal stage*, following the future restoration of Israel after Christ's second coming.

The first or elective stage began with Peter's visit to Cornelius and the acceptance of that first group of Gentiles into the Church. That was the occasion when "first God visited the Gentiles, to take out of them a people for his name," using Peter as His chosen instrument in thus "opening the door of faith unto the Gentiles" for the first time. This elective stage of Gentile visitation and outgathering is still going on, and will continue until the Lord returns. It is in this period that the Church plays its part in the divine program of missions. God is still, through His missionary messengers, pursuing His world-wide visit to the nations, not with the purpose of their national conversion and the bringing in of a millennium of peace and righteousness on earth through a transformation of the present political and social order into the kingdom of God on earth, as some are disposed to think, but rather with the purpose of "taking out of" all those nations "a people for his name," to comprise the true Church or Bride of Christ made ready for His return.

This new chapter in the divine program constitutes an

interruption, so to speak, in God's dealing with national Israel, a kind of parenthesis in Jewish history for the period of the Church age, or the interval between the ascension and second coming of Christ. Its introduction brought perplexity and questioning in the minds of the leaders of the early church, all of whom as yet were Jews. They of course recognized that Gentiles as well as Jews were included in God's provision and offer of salvation. This truth had been clearly set forth in the Old Testament Scriptures, it had been confirmed by the Lord Jesus, and Peter himself had declared it in his sermon at Pentecost. In point of fact, moreover, Gentiles had already been welcomed among the Jewish believers. These converts, however, had as yet been received as proselytes to the Jewish faith, and accordingly had undergone the Jewish rite of circumcision. But what was new and strange to the Jewish Christian leaders was the idea of preaching the Gospel directly to the Gentiles and receiving them into the Church on an equal standing with the Jewish believers, apart from any conformity to the rites and ceremonies of Judaism.

A wide and deep gulf had hitherto separated the Jews and the heathen Gentiles, and social and religious intercourse with Gentiles had been strictly forbidden all Jews and was rigidly shunned by them. The Church truth later revealed through the apostle Paul of the breaking down by God of the middle wall of partition between Jew and Gentile believers, so that "the Gentiles should be fellowheirs, and of the same body, and partakers of his promise in Christ by the gospel" (Eph. 2:14; 3:6), had as yet not been apprehended by Peter and the other apostles. Accordingly the Lord had to prepare Peter for his visit to Cornelius by overthrowing his firmly rooted Jewish prejudices which would have made any intimate social contact with this ceremonially unclean Gentile and his household repulsive and altogether unthinkable. It was with this purpose in mind that He gave to His Jewish apostle that vision on the housetop at Joppa.

While some may regard the "trance" into which Peter fell as nothing more than a grotesque dream, it in reality bears evidence of being a symbolic vision expressly designed to impart to Peter an understanding of this new departure in God's redemptive program for the Church age. That vessel "as it had been a great sheet" let down from heaven to earth, filled with all kinds of unclean animals, and then caught up again to heaven, was a vivid picture of the Christian Church. For, let it be remembered, the Church was not earth-born, but was the mystical Body of Christ, composed of both Jewish and Gentile believers "born from above" and united in the Head through the Spirit of God. There was no Church until Christ came down in the Person of the Holy Spirit to be the center around whom the Church was formed. Within this Church were to be enclosed the cleansed men and women hitherto spiritually and morally unclean (see, for example, I Cor. 6:9–11), and including those accounted unclean as being "aliens from the commonwealth of Israel, and strangers from the covenants of promise." That process of outgathering and bringing in such souls through the world-wide proclamation of the Gospel will continue until the number of the elect is accomplished and the Church (*ecclesia*—called-out company) is complete at the appearing of the Lord in glory (I Thess. 4:17), whereupon it will be caught up again into heaven, even as was the "great sheet" of Peter's vision.

This gap in Jewish national history is thus by no means an empty blank, but is pregnant with significance for the Gentile world. Yet far from its meaning the setting aside of God's purposes for Israel, the Scriptures make perfectly clear that upon the completion of the Church or Body of Christ and the return of the Lord, there is to be a resumption of God's dealing in grace with His ancient people "to whom pertaineth the adoption, and the glory, and the covenants, and the giving of the law, and the service of God, and the promises" (Rom. 9:4).

For confirmation of this order of God's redemptive dealings with Israel and the Gentiles we have but to turn to Paul's Epistle to the Romans, where in chapters nine to eleven the apostle sets forth impressively the successive stages of Israel's spiritual history, and shows clearly the bearing of it all upon the spiritual welfare of the rest of mankind. His line of reasoning is briefly as follows. God gave to the Jewish nation the promise of the Messiah. That promise was made good and the Messiah came, but Israel as a nation rejected Him. This did not mean that God had failed, nor yet that Israel's peculiar position before Him was done away with. In fact there was actually an election within the nation which *did* accept Christ, and in them God's promises were being fulfilled. But God's offer of salvation was extended to all men, and if the Jew rejected it and thus found himself for the time outside the favor of God, while the Gentile accepted it and entered upon the blessings of the Gospel, then the unfortunate result to the Jew was his own fault and could not be charged against God. Furthermore, the Jews' own prophets, Hosea and Isaiah, had foreseen and foretold this very situation (read in particular Rom. 9:22–33; 10:12–21).

But then the apostle raises the question, "Hath God cast away his people?" Is this rejection of Israel to be understood as a complete and final one? Is God done with Israel as a nation? At once he dismisses any conclusion of this kind with an emphatic "God forbid!" and proceeds to show that the rejection of Israel is even at present only partial, and that this

partial rejection is only temporary. He points to himself, a
saved Israelite, as evidence of a present election within the nation. He then goes on to affirm a future restoration of Israel
back to divine favor, and to make clear that God had a be-
neficent purpose in permitting this temporary setting aside of
national Israel. Through Israel's fall great spiritual riches have
come to the Gentile world, and if this be so, then the future
restoration of Israel will mean even greater riches.

To quote the apostle's precise statement, it reads as follows:
"I would not, brethren, have you ignorant of this mystery . . .
that a hardening in part hath befallen Israel, until the fulness of
the Gentiles be come in" (11:25). "I say then, Did they stum-
ble that they might fall? God forbid: but by their fall salvation
is come unto the Gentiles, to provoke them to jealousy. Now
if their fall is the riches of the world, and their loss the riches
of the Gentiles; how much more their fulness? For if the casting away of them is the reconciling of the world, what shall
the receiving of them be, but life from the dead?" (11:11,
12, 15, R.V.).

Turning back now to the fifteenth chapter of The Acts, let
us resume consideration of the speech with which James, as
presiding officer, closed the discussion by the Jerusalem council of the vexed question of the reception of Gentiles into the
Church. We have already called attention to the two stages of
God's redemptive dealing with the Gentile world, as clearly
indicated by the remarks of James, and we have dealt with
the first of these, the *elective stage*, ushered in by Peter's visit
to Cornelius and extending through the entire Church period
up to the return of Christ. But the second or *universal stage*
remains to be noted, for James after stating that "first God
visited the Gentiles, to take out of them a people for his name,"
goes on to say: "And to this agree the words of the prophets;

as it is written, after these things I will return, and I will build again the tabernacle of David, which is fallen; . . . and I will set it up: that the residue of men may seek after the Lord, and all the Gentiles, upon whom my name is called, saith the Lord, who maketh these things known from of old" (vs. 15, 16).

While James here cited "the prophets" as confirming his statement, he actually quotes from only one of them, namely, Amos (9:11, 12). He is affirming that at the end of the present elective stage of Gentile redemption, when through the world-wide preaching of the Gospel the Church, composed of all, whether Gentiles or Jews, who turn to Christ during this period, is completed, the Lord will return, even as He promised. His coming will be *first* to catch away the Church, which is His Body or Bride—an event commonly known as the Rapture (I Thess. 4:16, 17), and *then* in turn to fulfill to His earthly people Israel His promises under the Davidic covenant by "building again the tabernacle of David," restoring them as a nation in their own "promised land," and there setting up His throne and millennial kingdom over them (Lk. 1:32, 33).

Now it is to be acknowledged that Bible commentators do not all agree as to whether, or just how, the words of Amos here quoted fit into the sequence of events which James is outlining with reference to the Lord's dealings with Israel. The interpretation of the passage seems to hinge upon the words "after these things," for these words do not appear in the passage quoted from the prophet Amos, which reads: *"In that day* will I raise up the tabernacle of David. . . ."* But the argument of James, and the whole context, make it most natural to take James to mean that the prophet Amos' words (and the predictions of the other prophets as well) support the thought that it is following upon the completion and rapture of the Church that the Lord will fulfill His promise here mentioned concerning national Israel. And there are not a few commentators of high standing who hold to this view. We can quote here from only one of these, Professor J. M. Stifler, in his excellent volume entitled *The Acts of the Apostles*:

> When Peter's speech is explained and its significance shown, James brings in his quotation: "after these things I will return," etc. After what things? for the original is plural. After God's elective visit to the nations, and His creation of a church. It is not after the days of Amos but after the days of Israel's rejection and desolation and of a completed church. For the prophet did not use the words "after these things." They appear to belong to James. They are his explanation of the prediction in so far as they show to what period it applies. The time had not yet come for the fulfillment of this prediction. When the church has reached its complement then the Lord will return from visiting the Gentiles and rear up the fallen house of David, when not an elect number merely, but "all the Gentiles" shall seek the Lord, a blessing still in the future.

The present writer finds himself in hearty agreement with the view thus expressed by Stifler, and held by other scholarly expositors as well. But even if the words of Amos are not so to be interpreted, this would not at all contradict the program here set forth, as consisting of a present election from all nations of a people for His name, looking forward to a future time when "all Israel shall be saved." The evidence in favor of such a program is by no means limited to this passage in The Acts, and there are those who while not taking the view of it here advanced yet hold strongly to this plan of God as clearly unfolded in the chapters of Romans already cited, and in other Scriptures as well.

It is not our purpose to pursue the theme of this chapter beyond the point of the rapture of the Church at the return of Christ. Concerning the order of events which will then take place on the earth there is a wide divergence of view among prophetic teachers. Scores if not hundreds of books have been written on the subject, and numberless discussions and controversies carried on over various phases and details of the program of that period. While we recognize the worthiness of efforts to arrive at a correct understanding of all that pertains to eschatology, and have personally given time and thought to the subject, it is our firm conviction that the matter of supreme importance is to discern that the task set by Christ for His Church to accomplish during this dispensation is the evangelization of the entire world. This the inspired Word of God unmistakably reveals. And how we long that all Christians who hold the precious truth and cherish the blessed hope of the Lord's return, however they may differ in their interpretation of certain matters of detail or precise order, might join together in a wholehearted endeavor, by every means possible, to carry out our Saviour's last command!

Let it be noted right here that the Great Commission as stated in Acts 1:8 is not only a command, but is a prophecy as well, for it reads: "Ye SHALL be my witnesses . . . unto the uttermost part of the earth." Thus the Gospel *must* and *will* be carried to the ends of the earth before the Lord comes to take His Church away. What will take place after that, however important it may be, does not after all necessarily affect our duty to finish the task assigned to us now.

Mention may be made at this point of the view held by some that Colossians 1:23 teaches that the Gospel was preached to the entire world in the first generation of the Church. We must regard this interpretation of the passage as a straining of its natural meaning. The Revised Version's more accurate reading of the text is: ". . . the gospel which ye heard, which was preached in all creation under heaven." A similar statement occurs in verse six of the same chapter: ". . . whereof ye heard before in the word of the truth of the gospel, which is come unto you; even as it is also in all the word bearing fruit and increasing." The context makes it clear that Paul is here not intending to state how far the Gospel has gone, but is simply remarking, in the course of an exhortation to the Colossian Christians, that the Gospel which they had heard was the same Gospel that had been preached everywhere ("in all creation"). This is the sense given to the passage by standard commentaries, the expression "in all the world" being meant to be taken not literally, but hyperbolically, just as in other Scripture passages such general terms as "the world" and "all the city" are used. Moreover, the world that was known to the early apostles and covered by their preaching cannot intelligently be regarded as embracing the whole inhabited earth which, we believe, the Spirit of God has ever had in mind as the scope of the blessed Gospel's proclamation.

But further, if the literal interpretation of this Colossian passage is insisted upon, and the Gospel was actually preached to the whole world in that first generation, then the question arises, Why did not the end of the age come, and the Lord return? In Matthew's version of the Great Commission, Christ adds His promise to be with His missionaries "all the days, even unto the consummation of the age." He did not return at the end of the first generation, nor has He yet returned after nineteen hundred years, the obvious reason being that there were still millions then, and there are still millions today, who have never heard the Gospel. The clear implication is that "the consummation of the age" and the return of the Lord Jesus Christ will coincide with the completion of the assigned task of Gospel witnessing "unto the uttermost part of the earth."

Still another view which sadly militates against a united and wholehearted effort by the true Church of Christ to carry out to a finish in this day the evangelization of the world is that advanced by certain gifted teachers of prophecy for whom we have high regard, but with whom we must frankly disagree upon one important point. While holding firmly the truth of the Lord's premillennial coming, they yet relegate to a future company of Jews subsequent to the rapture of the Church the task of proclaiming the Gospel to the whole world, and accordingly they relieve the Church today of this responsibility. These teachers disclaim any relation between the completion of a world-wide witnessing of the Gospel and the Lord's return. While some who thus teach are missionary minded because of their love for the Lord, the natural result upon those who accept this teaching and apply it consistently is to cut the nerve of missionary concern and effort. What the Church fails to do in its day will be done by the "Jewish remnant" after the Church has been taken away!

We purposely refrain from any full discussion of this question here, although much could be said, for it is our earnest desire as far as possible to avoid all controversy in our advocacy of missions. Only this much we feel we must say, that we believe the prodigious achievement attributed to this "Jewish remnant" rests largely upon mere inference rather than upon any clear and explicit Bible statement, and that by this line of teaching the responsibility which Christ laid upon His Church for this age is shifted to others, wrongly and with most unfortunate results.

In saying this we would not be understood to mean that God's entire missionary program devolves upon the Church in this day, and that nothing is left for the future period following the rapture of the Church. This we have already indicated in our outline, early in the present chapter, of the two stages of God's redemptive dealings with the Gentiles. Upon the restoration of Israel following the second coming of Christ and the taking up of the Church, and on through the millennial reign of Israel's Messiah over the earth, His chosen and restored people will become a blessing to all the nations. It is to this period that the words of James apply: ". . . that the residue of men may seek after the Lord, and all the Gentiles, upon whom my name is called." This will be quite different from the earlier elective stage of "out-calling," for it will mean that the nations of the world as such will seek the Lord, as foretold in many Old Testament passages. In Isaiah 2:2 we read: "It shall come to pass in the latter days, that the mountain of Jehovah's house shall be established on the top of the mountains, and shall be exalted above the hills; and all nations shall flow unto it" (cf. Isa. 11:10; 60:5; 66:23; etc.).

We are careful to call attention to this later stage of the divine program in order to dispel misunderstanding which exists in the minds of some regarding the so-called premillennial view of the second advent. Those who, consistently with this view, hold that the goal of present-day missions is not world conversion, but rather world-wide witnessing or evangelization, are sometimes charged with pessimism in limiting the power and achievement of the Gospel in a way that is unworthy of it. Criticism of this kind really springs from a failure to grasp the true perspective of Scripture prophecy. If the present age or dispensation were the final one in God's great scheme, there would indeed be some ground for criticism or questioning of this kind. It needs to be seen that, as has already been said, the present is not the final stage of God's missionary program, but only a preliminary one, to be followed by a later stage subsequent to the second advent of our Lord. For example, the following prophecies, along with many others, are undoubtedly to be fulfilled: "Ask of me and I will give thee the nations for thine inheritance, and the uttermost parts of the earth for thy possession" (Psa. 2:8). "He shall have dominion also from sea to sea, and from the river unto the ends of the earth" (Psa. 72:8). "The earth shall be filled with the knowledge of the glory of Jehovah, as the waters cover the sea" (Hab. 2:4).

But these promises belong not to the present dispensation but to a future one, not to this elective stage of Gentile redemption but to the coming universal stage. And so the difference between the conflicting views regarding the objective of missionary effort is after all not so much a radical disagreement as to the ultimate goal, but rather a lack of common understanding as to the order and method of attaining that goal.

To revert to that teaching which sees no essential relation between the work of world-evangelization and the second advent of Christ, it has been said by one of its exponents that such a view would make Christ's coming a work of man's effort instead of an act solely of God's sovereign grace, and it is argued that because the time of His coming has been fixed by God from all eternity, therefore we can do nothing either to retard or to hasten it. This reasoning is to us far from sound or satisfying, for it would make God's dealings absolutely despotic and devoid of any regard for man's attitude and action, whether antagonistic or cooperative, and such we cannot believe to be the case. His divine sovereignty we reverently acknowledge, but that sovereignty has ever been wont to make use of man and of earthly factors in the working out of His purposes. Instance after instance of this can be cited in the Scriptures, as well as in all history.

It was surely a false conception of God's sovereignty that prompted the venerable moderator of that memorable Nottingham meeting of Baptist ministers to answer William

Carey's earnest appeal that something be done for the heathen world with the stern rebuke, "Sit down, young man. You are a miserable enthusiast to raise such a question. When God wants to convert the heathen He can do it without your help." While it is unquestionably true that the time of Christ's return has been fixed in the eternal counsel of our sovereign and omniscient God, yet that fact is by no means incompatible with the bringing about of the event through human processes and instrumentalities. Indeed, in the larger and Biblical view of God's sovereignty, these very processes and instrumentalities have all been ordained of God, who decrees not only the *end* but also the *means*. To omit the latter from the eternal plan of God is to fall into narrow and inadequate conceptions of the divine sovereignty.

Furthermore, God does not necessarily reckon time in the arbitrary terms of human days and years, but conceivably rather in terms of conditions and developments which make for the fulfillment of His eternal purpose. The "fullness of time" of our Saviour's first coming was brought about in this way, even though already fixed in God's predetermined plan, and He used not only devout servants of His, but also proud and bitter enemies as instruments in carrying out to the last letter His divine plan. Even so will it be with regard to the Saviour's second coming. It is frequently stated by certain prophetic teachers that all the various events and world conditions predicted in the Scriptures as having to be fulfilled prior to the return of Christ have taken place, and hence His coming may occur at any moment. But the fact remains that He has not yet come. Is this fact not a matter for serious thought, and is it not well to consider whether His delay may be because the task He assigned His followers has not yet been finished? Scripture pictures Him as the heavenly Bridegroom coming to take to Himself His chosen Bride. But the Bridegroom will surely not return for an incomplete Bride, and who will assert that the Bride or Church of Christ is to be composed wholly of saints from the favored lands where the Gospel has already been preached, and to the exclusion of any from the lands still unevangelized?

A well-known and discerning Christian leader who holds strongly that the Lord's second coming is unmistakably linked in God's Word with the completion of the task of world-wide Gospel witnessing, comments upon the command and *prophecy* of Acts 1:8 as follows: "If Christ should come today, then we would know that this prophecy has been fulfilled. But since He has not come, we know that it has not yet been fulfilled, and it is ours to study all the unreached parts of the earth and get the gospel to them immediately. . . . The Holy Spirit was sent for one great purpose in this age. As the Lord Jesus reported to the Father, 'I have finished the work Thou gavest me to do,' so will the Holy Spirit report to the Lord Jesus, 'I have finished the work Thou gavest me to do.' "

As to just what will constitute the fulfillment of the world-wide Gospel witness we do not presume to speak dogmatically. In the Great Commission, such words as "make disciples of all nations," "preach the gospel to every creature," and "be my witnesses unto the uttermost part of the earth," leave no doubt as to the program to which the Church is to address itself, and to pursue unremittingly until the Lord returns and brings it to an end. But what different factors may contribute to the carrying out of the witness, and precisely when and how it will be consummated, are questions which rest with the Lord and not with us His servants. We know of instances where the Gospel has reached out beyond where missionaries have personally gone, such outreach being through the printed page, or exploratory trips, or visits of individuals from those "regions beyond" to parts where missionary work exists, or possibly in other ways. Cases in point are the crossing over of Afghans, Baluchis, and Nepalese into India for trade or other purposes, and similarly of Tibetans and Mongols into China. And yet there are still large populations, including whole tribes, in some parts of the world which so far as we know have never yet heard the first sound of the Gospel.

Should not this solemn situation, coupled with the fact of the Lord's nonreturn, impel all true Christians, out of love for Him and for His appearing, and out of compassion for those who have never heard of Him, to put forth the greatest possible effort to extend the Gospel witness speedily to earth's utmost bounds? Sad to say, there are great numbers of professing Christians who show no concern whatever about the matter. And sadder still, there are even well-known prophetic teachers who pay little attention to missions. Large prophetic conferences have been held at which the various signs pointing to the near return of Christ were cited and exhaustively discussed, but where no mention was made of that most significant sign of all, the speeding up of God's appointed missionary program for this age. We well remember one particular instance when we listened to a masterful address on *The Signs of the Second Coming of Christ,* in which, however, no mention of the missionary sign was made. When we afterwards called the speaker's attention to this, sincerely thinking that the omission was purely from lack of time (for the hour was late), he expressed surprise and very frankly said that he did not believe missions had anything whatever to do with the return of Christ.

We are by no means disposed to overlook such signs as the steady increase of lawlessness, the rise of political dictatorships, the persecution of the Jews, the growing religious apostasy, and so on. But we would call attention to the fact that these are matters about which, despite our feeling of deep concern, we can do little or nothing, whereas promoting the spread of the Gospel to the ends of the earth is something in which all Christians can have an active and effective part.

Thus far in this chapter, in seeking to set forth the true goal of Christian missions today and the relation of the enterprise to Christ's second advent, the language of the Great Commission in its several renderings, and particularly the term "witness" as used in Acts 1:8, has been made the basis of our discussion. What has already been said might perhaps be regarded as sufficient treatment of the subject. But there is another term commonly used in Scripture to denote the objective of missions, and reference to it here, we believe, may contribute further to a clear understanding of the aim and end in view. This may involve some repetition of statements already made, but we trust not without profit. The term in mind is "harvest," and texts in which it occurs, e.g. John 4:35–38; Matthew 9:37, 38; Psalm 126:5, 6, will at once come to the reader's mind.

Perhaps no passage in all the Bible is more frequently quoted in missionary addresses than John 4:35, which reads: "Say not ye, There are yet four months, and then cometh the harvest? behold, I say unto you, Lift up your eyes, and look on the fields, that they are white already unto harvest." Extending the application of these words of our Lord from the little group of Jewish disciples whom He was addressing in Samaria to the Church at large, and from that local Sychar community to the whole world of today, let us consider the nature of the harvest of which He spoke, or in other words, the objective of the present missionary task. As to this, we find two widely differing views.

There are those who interpret the harvest in the final and complete sense of world conversion. In this view Christianity is conceived of as reaching out in ever-widening range and increasing influence, until by a steady, evolutionary process not only will individuals be converted, but entire communities and nations as well, society as a whole will be regenerated, moral evils overthrown, politics purged, wars outlawed, nations lifted to pure Christian ideals and conduct, and thus the present world order will gradually merge into the kingdom of God on earth. This conception quite naturally dictates a missionary policy which puts education, social service, industrialism, and the like in the foreground as contributory factors to that end.

There are two serious objections to the view that we may expect world conversion through the Church's missionary effort. First, this supposition is clearly out of harmony with many passages of Scripture, and second, it is not supported by the actual facts of the case.

The New Testament pictures the trend of the age in the very opposite direction from that which this view suggests. Wars and rumors of wars are to continue right on to the end. "Evil men and imposters shall wax worse and worse." "*In the last days* grievous times shall come," and this statement (II Tim. 3:1) is followed by a long list of grave moral and social evils which will be prevalent. Even religious life will have deteriorated in large measure into "a form of godliness, but having denied the power thereof" (II Tim. 3:5), and the last phase of the professing church in this age is that of the Laodicean church, the description of whose spiritual condition is pathetic in the extreme (Rev. 3:14–22). Surely the picture thus given in the Scriptures is anything but that of a regenerated world, or even a world progressing toward that state.

In the second place, no intelligent person can presume to see in developments during our own generation, or in prevailing conditions today, an upward trend toward such a social, moral, and spiritual Utopia. Is society being regenerated? Are moral standards becoming higher and purer? Are crime and delinquency on the steady decline? Are politics being purged of graft and corrupt practices? Nay, the very opposite of all this is plainly and undeniably in evidence.

One thing at least is clear, that if the harvest in view is world conversion, then that harvest must still be a very long way off, for it cannot be said with any semblance of truth that the mission fields of the world are anywhere near a condition which could be accurately described as "white already unto harvest" in that sense of the word. The stern fact faces us, despite the encouraging progress and cheering results of missionary work, that heathen the world over are increasing by natural propagation far more rapidly than Christians among them are increasing by regeneration, so that there are actually more heathen today than there were a century ago. That being so, how dark and discouraging is the outlook for missionaries if the full fruition of their efforts cannot be expected until some time in the remote future! It is this very thing, we believe, that has engendered indifference and apathy on the part of so large a section of the Church, since it is only natural to feel that for the promotion of an enterprise whose goal will not be reached for generations to come it does not really matter whether one does much or little.

But let us carry the argument a step further by considering the case of our home lands rather than the mission lands abroad. Take for example North America, which has had the Gospel and Christian advantages of many kinds for centuries, and is thus in an infinitely more favorable position than any of the mission lands. Can we point to one community, big or little, in this land of ours, where every person has already been converted, and a completely Christian town has been established? We fear such a place cannot be found. Then if after several hundred years of Gospel opportunity and effort, the first unit of this kind has yet to be produced, surely it is evident that any hope for the conversion of the entire globe by this process must be projected indefinitely into the future.

The other view of the harvest of which Jesus spoke is quite different. It regards that harvest not as a final and complete one in the sense of the conversion of the world, but as a first-fruits harvest, so to speak, or an outgathering of souls from all nations as the result of world-wide Gospel witnessing. And accordingly those holding this view make evangelism and the building up of indigenous churches their chief work.

Let us note the occasion and setting of these words of Jesus about harvest as serving to make plain what was in His mind. He had found that sinful woman at Jacob's well approachable, willing to listen, open to conviction, hungry-hearted for the Gospel message. Further, He envisaged behind her the town of Sychar with its many equally needy men and women, and the prospect of reaching them through her with the hope of bringing them also to repentance and salvation. Here was an open door, an opportunity for Gospel witnessing and soul winning to which He called the attention of His disciples in the words, "Lift up your eyes, and look on the fields, that they are white already unto harvest." He saw these souls, accessible and impressionable, as a field of ripened grain, a potential harvest ready for the reaping, and He longed that His disciples should share His vision and concern, and throw themselves into a prompt and wholehearted effort to make good that harvest before it was too late. Whether they actually did so seems doubtful, on the ground of their Jewish scruples and their lack of concern for souls. But the Lord Himself did so, tarrying there two days for that purpose, and with the result that "many believed on him." And yet this very statement clearly implies that *not all* the people of Sychar believed and were saved, which goes to show that Jesus used the word "harvest" not to denote a complete ingathering, but rather a partial outgathering as the result of Gospel effort.

Now this illustrates what "harvest" was intended to mean as applied to the larger work of the world-wide proclamation of the Gospel in this present age. The command was to witness for Christ "unto the uttermost part of the earth," to the end that thereby "a people for his name" might be called out of all nations to compose His Body, or Bride, for whom He will return. Thus the Church's task of world-evangelization is linked vitally with the blessed hope of the Lord's second coming. And here let it be noted that just as the thought of world conversion as the task enjoined is disheartening because it involves indefinite postponement of the end in view, so the thought of world-wide witnessing as the task is enheartening and inspiring, because of the practical possibility of its being carried to completion within the present generation. Indeed it should be obvious that this task *must* be accomplished within the limits of some one or other human generation. For example, the only generation of Christians that can evangelize the world of today is *this* generation of Christians, for when they pass away the same generation of heathen will also have passed away, and another world will be here, speaking in terms of its inhabitants.

Whatever may be true as to the opportunity which previous generations of Christians had of carrying out the Great Commission, it is certainly true that never did our Saviour's words "fields white unto harvest" find more full and forceful application than in our day and generation. The cumulative effect ot the long and faithful labors of the earlier missionaries, and the remarkable growth and development of the indigenous churches have brought the whole enterprise forward to a distinctly new stage. The attitude of the peoples and governments of mission lands has for the most part changed markedly for the better. The penetration of wholly unevangelized regions by brave pioneer bands has materially extended the frontiers of Christ's kingdom and contracted the unoccupied areas of the missionary world. The phenomenal advance in means of transportation has brought every part of the globe within swift and easy reach. New railroads and motor highways have been constructed in many lands, and the amazing multiplication of airways has revolutionized travel the world over. Material facilities of every kind have been multiplied to lend their aid. Radio broadcasting as an auxiliary missionary method has opened up well-nigh limitless possibilities. The translation and circulation of the Scriptures have steadily increased until the Bible, in whole or part, is now available in 1,066 languages and the Bible societies report yearly sales of 25,000,000 copies. For all these things one must fervently thank God.

While it is true that the recent global conflict has caused temporary interruption of normal activities in some fields, and new and serious problems in all of them, yet it is also true that God in His own matchless way has brought good out of evil, and has turned the war to the actual advantage of missions in a number of important respects. It is confidently expected that now, with the end of the war, there will be seen the greatest opportunity for advance and ingathering that the missionary enterprise has ever faced. What hope this inspires that at last, in this generation of ours, the long protracted task of taking the Gospel to the very ends of the earth may actually be carried out to a glorious finish, and the Lord Jesus may suddenly return to catch away His completed Church and beloved Bride!

Strangely enough, the opinion has been expressed in some quarters that belief in the soon return of Christ would tend to discourage missionary operations. Nothing could be farther from the truth. To the contrary it can be stated that the most earnest and aggressive evangelistic and missionary movements of our generation have been carried on by ardent believers in the "blessed hope." Moody, Torrey, Chapman, Sunday, and the other leading evangelists at home, and the many interdenominational foreign missionary agencies known as Faith Missions, with their several thousand workers, have all held this great truth and been inspired and stimulated by it. Mr. Moody testified that when it really gripped him, and he saw that Christ would not come until the last soul was saved to complete the full number of God's elect, it made him work three times harder, if perchance God might use him to the saving of the last soul to complete the Body of Christ. Hudson Taylor, the founder of the China Inland Mission, wrote: "If the Lord is coming soon, is this not a very practical motive for greater missionary effort? I know of no other motive that has been so stimulating to myself." And then he went on to cite several practical ways in which that "blessed hope" influenced him, the final one being that it gave him a deeper concern to extend the Gospel witness to the remotest corner of the world.

We have thus sought to make clear the vital relation between the Lord's Great Commission and the promise of His return. What has been said surely invests the work of world-evangelization with both solemn responsibility and glowing inspiration. Could anything be more inspiring to a missionary society than the hope that it might have the high privilege of penetrating the last unevangelized region of the world? Could anything be sweeter to the lonely pioneer on some far distant outpost of the field than the thought of perhaps being God's means of bringing in the last soul to complete the "people for his name" and thus preparing the way for his Lord's return? And what should stimulate zeal and sacrifice in the home churches more than to realize that their prayers and gifts for missions are contributing toward this great and glorious end? Do we cherish the "blessed hope"? Then let us obey Christ's last command. And when we pray, "Even so, come, Lord Jesus," let us ask ourselves whether we are doing all He expects of us toward bringing about the answer to that prayer.

VII

MEN AND MISSIONS

The Essential Elements of a Missionary Call

THERE are three great trunk lines for the outflow of missionary energy—by going, by giving, by praying. Hence there is a threefold appeal—for men to go, for stewards to give, for intercessors to pray. To these three factors in missions we shall now in turn give consideration.

First, there is the man factor. God might conceivably have chosen angels as His messengers to carry the Gospel to a lost world, and how gladly, we may be assured, they would have flown at His behest with the blessed evangel! But instead, He chose mortal men, bestowing upon them the high honor and privilege of being His co-workers in this glorious project.

That word in Ezekiel 22:30, "*I sought for a man,*" is an impressive reminder that God has *chosen* to make man an essential factor in the working out of His divine purposes, a fact at once solemnizing and inspiring. In that particular case the sad words follow, "but I found none." How almost unthinkable that Almighty God, the Creator of all men, should search among all His creatures, and the God of Israel among His chosen people, for just one individual to be His intermediary in His benevolent purpose toward that nation, but should search in vain! Alas, the same story has been repeated all down through the years that have followed, and that fact has been responsible for painfully long delays, and even periods of almost complete inaction, in the carrying out of the gracious desire and design of a loving God for the reclaiming of a world estranged from Him by sin.

Striking instances of God's seeking and using men as His chosen instruments lie all across the pages of Scripture. To Moses at the burning bush He said: "I have surely seen the affliction of my people which are in Egypt . . . and I am come down to deliver them. . . . Come thou therefore, and I will send thee . . . that thou mayest lead forth my people . . . out of Egypt." To Isaiah He cried from His heavenly throne, "Whom shall I send, and who will go for us?" To Jonah He gave the command, "Arise, go into Nineveh . . . and preach unto it the preaching that I bid thee." Repeatedly in the Old Testament we read that He "sent his servants the prophets, rising early and sending them" with messages to the rebellious and erring nation of Israel. Then the New Testament tells of the Lord Jesus' sending forth first the Twelve, and then the Seventy, and finally of His post-resurrection commissioning of the apostles and the entire Church to be His messengers in spreading abroad the good news of His salvation.

It is clear that the work of Gospel witnessing was not meant by Christ to be confined to any select coterie of persons holding official positions within the Church, but was to be shared by all believers according to their various capabilities and opportunities. Ephesians 4:11, 12 (R.V.) reads that the ascended Christ "gave some to be apostles; and some, prophets; and some, evangelists; and some, pastors and teachers; for the perfecting of the saints, unto the work of ministering, unto the building up of the body of Christ." This reading corrects the wrong impression conveyed by the King James Version that "the ministry" is confined to those holding such offices as apostle, prophet, evangelist, pastor, and teacher, and that the other members of the Church, the so-called laity, have no part in the work. No, these office-holders are simply meant to function in their respective capacities with a view to building up the Body of Christ, that is, all believers, and leading them in a corporate "work of ministering" in which every member has a part.

In one sense, then, every real Christian, or true member of the Body of Christ, is a missionary, a "sent one," sharing both the privilege and the responsibility of carrying out the Great Commission. But there is another sense in which the word "missionary" is generally used, as designating those who give themselves to the full-time service of carrying the Gospel to others, and particularly to foreign lands which have not been evangelized. It is to this aspect of the word "missionary" that we are here to give our thought.

Who are called to be missionaries? How is one to know whether he is called to go as a missionary? On what basis should the decision rest? In other words, what really constitutes a missionary call? These questions are constantly being asked by earnest young Christians. We have been faced with them repeatedly in Bible institutes, missionary conferences, and in other connections. They are admittedly important questions, and when honestly asked they call for sympathetic and painstaking consideration. Nothing could be more vital to any-one setting out for the mission field than to be clearly assured of the call and leading of the Lord in taking that step. Without such assurance one would be exposed to distressing doubts, and to the subtle insinuations of the Evil One, in confronting the many severe trials and tests which are inseparable from missionary life and labor. To quote the words of Hudson Tay-lor: "A missionary who is not clear on this point will at times be almost at the mercy of the great Enemy. When difficulties arise, when in danger or sickness, he will be tempted to raise the question which should have been settled before he left his native land: 'Am I not in my wrong place?' "

But widely differing views exist as to what constitutes a missionary call. There are many who seem not to have any clear view at all, and it must be said that there is a good deal of fog, illusion, and false sentiment about the question, and at times even evasion and insincerity. To attempt to settle it on the ground of one's *feeling called*, or *not feeling called*, is utterly to misconceive the whole matter. What, then, is to be regarded as the true nature and the right basis of a missionary call? We have no magic formula or patent prescription to offer. We simply turn with this problem, as with every other, to the Word of God for a solution. In this instance it is but natural that we turn in particular to The Acts as designed, we believe, to be an inspired manual for the guidance of the Christian Church in all that pertains to its missionary enterprise. We suggest that in the Macedonian vision and call given to the apostle Paul, God has furnished us with a clear and satisfactory model for a missionary call today. Let us then give it our careful attention as we find it recorded in chapter sixteen of The Acts.

One cannot read this chapter without being struck with the startling nature of the incident mentioned in verses six and seven. Paul with two companion workers is on his second missionary journey through Asia Minor, and they are about to enter the province of Asia when suddenly the Holy Spirit "forbids" them. Turning northward, "they assayed to go into Bithynia," another province, "but the Spirit suffered them not." Think of it! This was no company of slackers, or careless, worldly Christians, but of earnest, consecrated workers for the Lord, and bent on a tour of Gospel preaching. And yet they are twice peremptorily stopped by a divine prohibition.

What could it mean? Was it that there was no more need in Asia and Bithynia, that everyone there had been converted? Decidedly not, as is evidenced by the fact that Paul later on was led back by the Spirit to Asia, where he spent two whole years preaching in its capital city of Ephesus, and with the manifest approval and blessing of the Lord upon his ministry (see chapter nineteen).

What, then, did the Spirit of God mean by stopping these missionaries at the threshold of that province upon this earlier occasion? The inference is plain, namely, that He meant to insist on fair play, on an equal opportunity being given to hear the message of salvation, on placing no premium upon souls in one area and discount upon souls in another. Paul was proposing to go a second time over ground which he had already covered once, unmindful of the fact that just across the Ægean lay another country, indeed a whole continent, which had not yet had its first opportunity of hearing the Gospel. Although he was the foremost missionary of his day, and the greatest missionary statesman of any day, and had an exceptionally broad missionary vision, yet even he had never lifted up his eyes to see beyond the confines of his own continent. God had to take this means of further enlarging his vision, and bringing him to think not merely in provincial or even continental terms, but rather in terms of the whole world. The Holy Spirit's vision far outdistanced Paul's. Moreover, He envisaged the dominant place Europe was destined to hold, and the powerful influence that continent was to wield, in the affairs of the entire world of the future, and this made it the more urgent that the light of the Gospel be given her.

What a lesson there is here not only for the apostle Paul but also for every Christian worker, and every Christian believer! God calls upon His people to expand their contracted horizons, to enlarge their narrow sympathies, to extend their limited efforts, and to become world Christians in their thinking and acting.

Someone has said that no person has a right to hear the Gospel twice until everyone has heard it once. That may be an extreme statement, and need not be taken too literally, yet it does express a true principle which ought to govern Christian work, for it emphasizes God's impartial love for all men, irrespective of clime, or race, or color, and His desire that the Bread of Life be distributed impartially and equally to all. In the instance before us, He deliberately called a temporary halt in a home missionary campaign, so to speak, until the neglected foreign end of the one great missionary enterprise was brought up into line. We believe there are many cases in which He would have the same thing done today.

The incident before us is also a solemn reminder of how inadequate human wisdom is at its best for the direction of missionary policies and operations. Despite Paul's outstanding leadership and ripe experience, as well as his utter sincerity of motive and his deep devotion, he at this juncture would have taken a wrong step had not the faithful Spirit of God overruled and corrected him. How constantly do missionaries, whether young or old, or howsoever gifted and experienced they may be, need to depend from first to last, and in matters of every kind, upon a higher wisdom than their own, and to wait humbly and continuously on the Lord for guidance!

And now proceeding on to verses eight and nine, we face the question of the "man of Macedonia" who appeared to Paul in this vision. Who was this man? Was he a real man? Did the apostle later meet him when he reached Macedonia? These questions have often been asked and discussed. In our opinion the "man of Macedonia" was not an actual person, but was rather a personification or visual portrayal of the spiritual need of Macedonia. Just as the portrait of George Washington flashed upon the screen would at once bring to mind the United States of America, of which he ever stands as a symbol, so the appearing of this man to Paul in a vision was God's way of calling attention to the land of Macedonia in its dire, unmet spiritual need. And his cry, "Come over into Macedonia and help us" was a dramatic and arresting missionary plea. The message to Paul and his companions was, MACEDONIA NEEDS THE GOSPEL. Macedonia, it is true, had much to her credit, and of which she might be justly proud. She had her Grecian art, philosophy, and religion; her schools and temples; her poets, sages, and orators. But Macedonia had no Gospel, no saving message: she needed Jesus Christ, and the mute appeal of that vision was, "Bring us the Saviour."

Are not the heathen and Moslem lands of the world today the very counterpart in this respect of Macedonia of Paul's day? China, Japan, India, and other countries have similarly much that is noteworthy and commendable in their national history, their literature, their arts and industries, their vast store of empirical knowledge along many lines. But they have no Gospel, no saving message, unless taken to them from the God-favored lands of the West.

Will civilization meet the spiritual need of these lands? Assuredly no! Railroads, motor cars, electric light, sewing machines, fountain pens, and a multitude of other importations from the West do not bring their peoples one whit nearer salvation. And while the introduction of more up-to-date Western business methods, wider city streets, better sanitation, new styles of apparel, and modern conveniences and mechanical devices of many kinds may be of advantage in raising the scale of living, improving domestic conditions, stimulating trade, and increasing opportunities for money making and the pursuit of pleasure, these things do not of themselves minister in the least to the souls of men. Furthermore, a very serious indictment can be brought against civilization on the score of its baneful influence upon the peoples of mission lands through the flood of moral vices it has introduced, and the shockingly bad example many of its representatives have set by their shameful conduct. It is a sad fact that where the East and the West have come together, apart from missionary contact, the result in the main has been to impart to each other their respective vices rather than their virtues. And if anything more requires to be said, we need only point to the ghastly spectacle which World Wars I and II, waged between the leading civilized nations of the world, have presented before the eyes of the heathen. No, civilization falls woefully short of meeting the need of pagan and Moslem peoples.

Will education meet their need? Here again the answer must be an emphatic NO. Its attempt to do so has signally failed. Where Western governments have conducted educational programs in lands under their control, but have excluded Christian teaching from their curricula, the result has been to put new and formidable weapons into the hands of those who resent their rule and cherish the hope of overthrowing it. Years ago a religious census of 5,000 Japanese students in the Tokyo University, conducted on Western lines, told the following amazing tale: Confucianists, 6; Shintoists, 8; Buddhists, 300; Christians, 30; atheists, 1,500; agnostics, 3,000. Here is a shocking but true sample of what liberal education leads to, when devoid of genuine Christian teaching and influence. The same thing is all too plainly in evidence in our own land.

No, neither civilization, nor education, nor anything else but the Christian Gospel can meet the fundamental need of the lands that are the counterpart today of Macedonia in Paul's day. *They need, they must have Jesus Christ.*

But now a step further. To say that Macedonia *needed* the Gospel is not to claim that Macedonia *wanted* the Gospel. We do not read that when Paul crossed the Ægean to Macedonia he found a crowd of seeking souls eagerly awaiting him on the shore, or when he entered Philippi. Nor is this the experience of the missionary today in arriving in any foreign field. But this fact is not surprising, nor should it be discouraging. How could the Macedonians *want* something of which they had never heard? Thus the beginning of missionary work in that virgin soil was not spectacular, but small and humble, and God's messengers had to go patiently forward, step by step, praying constantly for the Spirit's guidance. This they did, and with confidence, assured that God had called and led them, and that therefore their coming could not be in vain.

Nor were they left long without visible evidence of this fact, for only a few days passed before they were brought in touch with Lydia, "whose heart the Lord opened, that she attended unto the things which were spoken of Paul," and became the first European convert to Christ. The Lord does not thrust out His servants on some futile project or mere peradventure. When He gave Paul that vision at Troas, His Spirit was already at work in Macedonia making ready for his coming. So it is today in the case of every missionary whom God calls and sends forth. He finds that God has gone before him, preparing the way and opening the hearts of "certain men and women" to receive his message, so that sooner or later visible fruit appears to cheer him. This we can confidently affirm on the ground of our own and others' experience in pioneer fields. And what a blessed experience it is to be God's connecting link with precious souls in heathendom whose hearts God opens to the Gospel, and to be the means of leading them into its glorious light!

Proceeding now to verse ten, we find in the reaction of Paul and his companions to that Macedonian vision definite light on the question of the missionary call. The verse reads: "After he had seen the vision, immediately we endeavored to go into Macedonia, assuredly gathering that the Lord had called us for to preach the gospel unto them." Let us take its phrases one by one.

"*After he had seen the vision . . .*" That simply means, "after God had brought to Paul's attention certain facts to which he had never before given any thought." There in another continent was a land which as yet had not had its first opportunity to hear of the only Saviour, while he was confining his thought and efforts to people who had already heard. It was not that all who had heard the message has accepted it, or even that every individual in Asia and Bithynia could be said to have been contacted. But they had at least to some extent been enlightened, whereas not a ray of Gospel light had as yet penetrated Macedonia. Now this is just the "vision" the Lord would bring before His people today of lands across the sea, where millions still live in heathen darkness without ever having heard of His salvation. Nor can we plead ignorance of this fact as Paul might perhaps in some measure have done in his day, because of the vastly greater knowledge we possess concerning conditions in other parts of the world, as well as our far better facilities for reaching them. The facts about the heathen lands of today we well know, or we can readily learn if we want to know them, and these facts become the finger of God pointing out our responsibility and duty.

"*Immediately we endeavored to go into Macedonia.*" What a magnificent response was this to the call of God! No offering of excuses or alibis! No arguing about "work enough to do at home"! No pleading of personal reasons why *they* could not leave the home land, and attempting to shift upon *others* the responsibility of going! And how eternally thankful to God we should be for all this, and that Paul "was not disobedient to the heavenly vision," but *went!* For can we ever forget that his thus taking the Gospel to Europe was the beginning of the spiritual enlightenment and transformation of that continent whence came our ancestors, and that the difference between what we are today and what our then pagan forbears were can be traced back to these pioneer labors of that noble missionary, the great Apostle of the Gentiles? Then unless we Christians are content to be known as ingrates, we shall follow Paul's example in doing our utmost to speed forward the blessed evangel which has changed our lives. We shall eagerly give it to the continents whose peoples still lie in darkness and the shadow of death because they have never been given the Light of Life.

But the language of this verse calls for still closer scrutiny. Note first the word *"immediately."* It speaks of prompt obedience to the call of God, no dillydallying, no procrastination, but a beginning to act, the moment His voice is heard. We are aware of the possibility of running ahead of the Lord, but there is the even greater danger of lagging behind, and putting off the doing of His bidding when once He has spoken. We can recall many tragic instances of this failure, where young Christians have heard the call of God and seen the vision of His plan for them, but have allowed one thing or another to keep them from rendering prompt, implicit obedience, with the sad result that the vision has faded, they have lost out spiritually, and in later years have been filled with remorse as they recalled the time when God spoke but they failed to heed and act, and thus missed His best for their lives. As we value our souls, let us beware of giving way to the subtle temptation to procrastinate and delay in taking the first definite step forward along the path which He has revealed to us.

Then follow the words, *"we endeavored to go."* They express a genuine purpose and honest effort to go, which is so different from that passive "willingness" that many young people have professed, but without treating the matter seriously or taking any practical steps toward going. It is sadly possible to be stirred emotionally by a missionary appeal to the extent of raising the hand in response, but without any crystallizing of the gesture in definite purpose and advance. In not a few cases, we fear, such outward sign of response is a mere gesture to relieve the feelings of the moment, and perhaps with the secret hope that the Lord will not press the issue. The impression made is thus only superficial and transient and soon passes off and is forgotten.

The meeting with hindrances in the way of carrying out one's resolve to be a missionary should not be taken as indicating that it is not the Lord's will for one to go, and thus lead to discouragement and the abandonment of the aim. Obstacles are not surprising but rather to be expected, as being both the devil's attempt to hinder, and the Lord's means of testing the sincerity and strength of one's purpose and preparing one for the even greater difficulties and testings which will have to be faced on the field.

The next phrase, *"assuredly gathering that the Lord had called us . . ."* is especially significant. "Assuredly gathering" is not the language of mere sentiment, but rather of thoughtful reasoning and logical conclusion. Indeed it is almost the language of mathematics, which puts two and two together and figures that the result is unquestionably four. The idea of some people that a missionary call is a matter of the emotions is quite erroneous. God can, of course, guide us through our emotions, if He so chooses, for He has given them to us. But He can just as truly guide us through our reasoning faculties, when these are surrendered to Him. He thus guided Paul in the instance before us. Two doors before him had been shut in close succession, and then came the vision of Macedonia so strikingly brought to his notice. Here was a great need as yet wholly unmet, whereas Asia and Bithynia, although still needy, had already had at least some opportunity to hear of Christ. Putting these facts together and prayerfully pondering them, Paul and his companions were led to conclude ("assuredly gather") that God's will for them was to proceed to Macedonia. It was a sane deduction from facts, reached by minds and hearts fully yielded to the Lord and under His control. Nor were they mistaken in their reasoning and conclusion, as the sequel clearly proved.

The truth which we would emphasize, as made clear by this Macedonian incident, is that a genuine missionary call rests upon a basis not of feeling but of fact, just as our salvation itself does. There may be, and indeed *should* be, feeling associated with it, but that feeling is the effect of the call, and not its foundation. Now there are two great basic facts which underlie a true and satisfactory missionary call, and these are well illustrated by the Macedonian vision given to the apostle Paul. For that was a twofold vision, combining both heavenly and earthly factors.

First, it was a heavenly vision. Of that there can be no question. It came from God, who spoke and gave to Paul a revelation of His will, so that the apostle's words "I was not disobedient to the heavenly vision" apply to this vision just as truly as to that earlier vision to which he alluded in his defense before Agrippa (Acts 26:19). The first essential factor of a genuine missionary call is *a revelation of the divine will.* How is one to get this? Must he have repeated to him a vision similar to that of Paul? Is he to expect some spectacular drama and audible voice from heaven? Not at all. The revelation of the divine will is to be found in the inspired Word of God which He has given us, so that we no longer need a special visitation from heaven such as came to Paul. As someone has put it, "The missionary call now is not a *voice,* but a *verse.*" As we have seen in preceding chapters, God's Word makes crystal clear His will that the Gospel be taken to all mankind, and it should be the earnest concern of every child of God to find out, and then fulfill, the part which is ordained for him in this great undertaking.

In the second place, it was an earthly vision. Macedonia was not a myth or a fancy: it was a place on the map. It was a country peopled with souls who were without the Gospel and needed it. If Paul had not yet heard of such a country, or had given no thought to it, God thus brought it to his notice and made it his business to give attention to it. This gives us the second essential factor of a true missionary call, which is *a revelation of human need.* How is one to get this? Obviously by acquainting himself with the salient facts concerning the different parts of the world, and particularly as regards their supply and need of Gospel light. The facilities for learning these facts are today so abundant that no intelligent Christian has any reasonable excuse for remaining ignorant.

It has been truly said that "a need, knowledge of that need, and ability to meet that need constitute a call." It was this *logic of facts* that appealed to Keith Falconer, that heroic Scottish nobleman who blazed the Gospel trail into the "ignored peninsula" of Arabia. Said he: "While vast continents still lie shrouded in almost utter darkness, and hundreds of millions suffer the horrors of heathenism and Islam, the burden of proof rests upon you to show that the circumstances in which God has placed you were meant by Him to keep you out of the foreign mission field." James Gilmour, the brave pioneer among the nomads of Mongolia, spoke in words no less forceful and convicting: "To me the question was not 'Why go?' but 'Why not go?' Even on the low ground of common sense I seemed called to be a missionary. For is the kingdom not a harvest field? Then I thought it only reasonable to seek the work where the work was most abundant and the workers were fewest."

If now we put together these two aspects of the Macedonian vision which have been set forth, the heavenly and the earthly, the divine and human factors, we have the sound Scriptural basis for a true missionary call. Such a call rests not on feeling or sentiment, but on two great facts: first the fact of God's will as revealed in the Word, and then the fact of human need as revealed in the world. Only upon an honest and serious consideration of these two facts can any Christian reach an intelligent and conscientious decision as to where and what his part should be in helping to carry out the one great business of the Church of Christ on earth, the giving of the Gospel to the whole world.

The call to military service furnishes a fitting illustration of what we are seeking to emphasize respecting missionary service. This country when at war declares a draft of man power, in terms of which every man of military age and fitness is conscripted for active service. The norm is to go, not to stay. The only honorable exempts from going are those disqualified for overseas service, or those who can serve their country's cause better by remaining at home. Exactly so should it be in the

Church's missionary war. In view of Christ's imperative "GO" and the overwhelmingly greater need in the foreign fields than at home, loyalty to Him and love for lost souls constitute a compelling claim upon all Christians whose age, health, qualifications, and providential circumstances admit of it, to answer the call in person and "endeavor to GO," while all others should "GO" by prayer and purse, to the full measure of their ability.

One word ought perhaps to be added to clear up a point of honest perplexity which may still remain in some minds. All that has been said thus far relates to the missionary call *in general.* But it may be asked, "Am I not to expect a *personal* call, and a call to some particular field and work?" Our reply is, "Yes indeed, but not until you become eligible for this." Only those may expect such special call who have taken the proper attitude toward the general call (the Great Commission), and placed themselves unreservedly at the Lord's disposal. It is just as it was in the case of your salvation. You did not see your individual name in the Gospel invitation or call of the Saviour, but you saw the word "whosoever," and when you responded to that general call and appropriated it for yourself, then the Holy Spirit particularized the call to you and gave you the assurance of your personal salvation. Even so, it is only when you have accepted the general call, or command, of the Great Commission, and acknowledged your responsibility to it, that you become eligible for a personal call to some particular field and post. But to the one who has surrendered unreservedly to the Lord, with the single desire to know His will, and to fill the place and do the work that He desires, wherever and whatever that may be, certain guidance will surely be given, and everything will be made clear in due time, even down to the smallest detail. Ample assurance of this fact is found in Psalm

25:9; 32:8; John 7:17, and many other precious texts. When we can truthfully say with Eliezer of old, "I being in the way," then we can confidently add as he did, "the Lord led me" (Gen. 24:27).

There is nothing more vitally important for each of us than to know the will of God for our life; and there is no joy, or peace, or satisfaction so great as to be completely in that will, and in His appointed place for us, in the blessed work of carrying the message of eternal salvation to a lost world. "Lord, what wilt thou have me to do?"

VIII

MONEY AND MISSIONS

Bible Light on Missionary Stewardship

HAVING dealt with the man factor in missions, and faced the question of the call for recruits to go, we now proceed with the money factor, or the question of the financial support of missions. That money is needed, as well as men, for the task of evangelizing the world is altogether obvious. Equipping and sending out missionaries to distant lands, and supporting them and their activities there, is a costly business. Along with the appeal, therefore, for men and women to *go in person*, comes the companion appeal to the Lord's people at home to *go by purse*, that is to say, to make possible by the consecration of their financial means the going forth of those who have consecrated their lives to the work of carrying the Gospel to the unevangelized abroad.

This need brings before us the subject of Christian stewardship in the realm of money or material things, a theme of great practical importance, and one about which the Word of God has a great deal to say. Indeed it will surprise those who have not given the matter any serious thought to find how much the Bible talks about money. Nor is this strange but only natural, since God's Word deals with everything that has to do with human life, and certainly money is one such thing.

Beginning with the Old Testament, we turn first to Psalm 24:1: "The earth is the Lord's, and the fulness thereof." This verse, we fear, is too commonly taken as merely a choice bit of Hebrew poetry. It needs to be regarded more seriously as the plain statement of a literal fact. The world, with all that it contains, belongs to God, and He has never abrogated His claim upon any part of it. It does not belong to any nation or group of nations, nor yet to the millionaires, nor even the multimillionaires. We have become accustomed to talking in terms of ownership of property and personal effects, but in reality no man *owns* anything. We simply have the use of what we call our possessions, for the brief term of our earthly life at longest, and then we must relinquish them all. "We brought nothing into this world, and it is certain we can carry nothing out" (I Tim. 6:7). It is fundamental to a right understanding of stewardship that we realize and accept this great fact. Only by the favor of Almighty God do we possess anything, and He can take it from us at any moment that He chooses so to do.

Apropos of what has just been said is a remark by the late Dr. A. J. Gordon about gifts to Christian causes in the form of bequests. His words may seem to some as rather ironical, but they are worthy of serious reflection. "Is it not distinctly affirmed in Scripture," said he, "that we must all appear before the judgment-seat of Christ, that *every one may receive the deeds done in the body?* Why, then, should Christians so industriously plan that their best deeds should be done *after they get out of the body?* Is there any promise of recompense for this *extra corpus* benevolence?" Much loud commendation is given to "munificent bequests" to the Lord's work by persons who have lived in the selfish enjoyment of their wealth, holding on to the entire principal as long as they could, and only when they could keep it no longer have "left" it to a good cause. Would it not in many cases have been more beneficial to the cause in question and more pleasing to the Lord, as well as a rich spiritual blessing to the donors themselves, had their gifts, or a substantial portion of them, been made while they still lived?

God's dealings with Israel under the Mosaic law furnish the abiding principles of His government for all time. Turning, for example, to the twenty-fifth chapter of Leviticus we find set forth very clearly His regulations regarding His people's relation to property, hired labor, interest charges, and the like. Verse twenty-three serves as a starting point. It reads: "The land shall not be sold for ever: for *the land is mine;* for ye are strangers and sojourners with me." Now God had promised Canaan to Abraham and his seed forever (Gen. 12:7; 13:15; 17:8). But they were given to understand that this did not confer upon them absolute ownership, but only leasehold rights. This fact He confirmed by that remarkable system of sabbatisms which He enacted—the seventh day, the seventh week, the seventh month, the seventh year, and finally the fiftieth or jubilee year which followed the seventh period of seven years. The laws concerning each and all of these were designed to teach a very important lesson as to the relation of God to what men call their property. Every Israelite was reminded that the land which he tilled belonged, not to himself, but to God. That his time belonged to God was emphasized by God's requiring the absolute consecration to Him of every seventh day, and that the land belonged to God was made clear by His similar claim that the land be not tilled but given rest every seventh year, and also every fiftieth year besides.

Verse twenty of this chapter anticipates the natural question which would arise in the mind of an Israelite as to how he could subsist under the rigid restrictions that had been imposed: "If ye shall say, What shall we eat the seventh year? behold, we shall not sow, nor gather in our increase: Then I will command my blessing upon you in the sixth year, and it shall bring forth fruit for three years." In this practical way the Hebrews were taught that "man doth not live by bread alone, but by every word that proceedeth out of the mouth of God," and a vital truth for all time was emphasized, namely, that the soul of all true religion is implicit faith toward God, which of course assumes glad response to all His commands and revealed will.

Other verses in the chapter lay down regulations governing land transfer and forced labor induced by debts incurred, loans to the poor and interest thereon, and other community transactions. The culminating and most arresting thing is the provision by which in every jubilee (fiftieth) year all debts, labor contracts, and real estate transfers were cancelled, and the whole land reverted to its original plan of distribution among the various tribes and their families according to their numbers. The intended effect of all these regulations was to impose a powerful check upon man's natural covetousness and insatiate greed for riches; to maintain, as far as possible, an equal distribution of wealth by preventing excessive accumulation of property or money by the few, at the cost of impoverishing the many; and to inculcate a feeling of unselfish interest in and consideration for others, especially the poor and unfortunate, and that spirit of "godliness with contentment" which is "great gain."

That such legal enactments are practicable under the conditions of modern life, or that they are morally binding today, is not at all our contention, although present-day legislators could well afford to ponder these God-given laws for Israel, as furnishing the basic principles of all sound legislation in every day, and more particularly as touching the ever-recurring problem of effecting an equitable distribution of wealth and preventing dangerous extremes of either riches or poverty.

The point, however, that we wish to stress is the very practical and searching lesson which these regulations laid down by God for His ancient people are designed to teach all Christians today as to right and wrong conceptions and use of the material assets which He has entrusted to them. While it is true that they are not under the exacting laws imposed on Israel of old, yet they should be constrained by the law of the Spirit of grace operating within their hearts, as were those first believers after Pentecost, of whom we read that "neither said any of them that ought of the things which he possessed was his own," and who placed all they had at the Lord's disposal for the promotion of His cause.

Passing on to the eighth chapter of Deuteronomy we find another exhortation and warning from the Lord to His people Israel just before they were to enter the Promised Land. He reviews His gracious dealings with them all through their wilderness journeyings, and dwells upon the better things in store for them in that good land into which He was taking them. But then He earnestly warns them of the danger, when they should become prosperous and wealthy, of forgetting their obligations to Him as the source and giver of all material blessings. "Beware that thou forget not the Lord thy God, . . . lest when thou has eaten and art full, and hast built goodly houses, and dwelt therein; . . . and thy silver and thy gold is multiplied, and all that thou hast is multiplied; then thine heart be lifted up, and thou forget the Lord thy God, . . . and thou say in thine heart, My power and the might of mine hand hath gotten me this wealth" (vs. 11–18).

Are not these solemn words of warning quite as applicable to God's people today, and quite as much needed as in the day in which they were first given? How many are the instances in which Christians who have been conscientious and faithful in their walk and witness for Christ during years of modest income have become much less so when their financial standing has substantially improved! Many an one who when poor was careful always to set aside a tenth of his small earnings for the Lord, even though this necessitated rigid economy or actual sacrifice, has after acquiring riches drifted into neglecting the tithe, as the things that catered to his pride or pleasure have gradually absorbed his attention. "The tragedy of money making," writes a thoughtful observer, "is that it becomes an end in itself instead of a means to an end. When a man begins to amass wealth, it is a question as to whether God is going to gain a fortune or lose a man."

Akin to the thought of this Deuteronomy passage is that of another in Proverbs (3:9) which says: "Honor the Lord with thy substance, and with the first fruits of all thine increase." Now there are various ways in which a Christian can honor his Lord—by his consistent conduct, by his faith in God's promises, by his zeal in witnessing, by his deeds of kindness, and so on. But mention is here made of still another and very distinctive way in which the child of God can honor (or dishonor) the Lord, namely, in his relation to money or its equivalent in property. It is to be feared that some Christians who in these other ways are honoring their Lord are yet failing to do so in this particular sphere. With some the money test would seem to be the severest of all.

In the text just quoted, the admonition is followed with a promise of reward of a material kind for such honoring of God with one's substance: "So shall thy barns be filled with plenty, and thy presses shall burst out with new wine." This Old Testament promise of material recompense for obedience is not found in the New Testament. God's children under grace are not guaranteed temporal enrichment but are taught to value spiritual riches, and to set their affection "on things above, not on things on the earth." There is, for example, that lovely assurance of James 2:5, "Hath not God chosen the poor of this world rich in faith, and heirs of the kingdom which he hath promised to them that love him?" Nevertheless it is true that God still controls all material things, and reserves to Himself the right to grant financial prosperity to whom He will. He is pleased at times to bestow wealth upon certain of His children, that they might be His channel for the relief of His poor saints or the support of His Gospel enterprise. One notable example of this fact was the Honorable Alpheus Hardy of Boston, who used his consecrated money to befriend and educate a Japanese waif who had contrived to escape from his native land as a stowaway on an American schooner for Shanghai, and thence worked his way to the United States. In this way Mr. Hardy provided Japan with one of her greatest native Christian apostles in the person of Joseph Hardy Neesima. But this is only one instance among many of Christians who have honored God with their substance, and whom God in turn has honored with increasing riches to be spent for His cause and glory. Other refreshing cases in our own day come to mind in which business acumen and money-making ability have been turned to account for God rather than for personal advantage, so that steadily mounting profits are zestfully devoted to missions instead of being spent for a finer home and added luxuries, or hoarded in a swollen bank account. Thus God is honored by His loyal servants who have learned the better way of laying up treasure in heaven rather than on earth.

Turning now to the prophecy of Haggai, we come upon most heart-searching utterances regarding money and its relation to the kingdom of God. Haggai 2:8 reads, "The silver is mine, and the gold is mine, saith the Lord of hosts." Again and again is this verse quoted as an assurance that a rich Heavenly Father will furnish needed funds for His trusting children and their work for Him. And quite similarly are quoted God's words in Psalm 50:10, that "Every beast in the forest is mine, and the cattle upon a thousand hills." Now we would be far from depriving any needy and trusting children or servants of the Lord of the comforting assurance that He will supply their every lack out of His boundless storehouse. There is indeed a sense in which these texts may legitimately be thus applied, in keeping with many other Scriptures which give the same assurance. But the context clearly shows that the primary meaning of both passages is altogether different from this. In both cases the words are spoken by God to His people in tones not of comfort but of stern rebuke.

To take first the passage in the Psalms, He is here protesting against the mere form of worship without the heart being in it. Israel was continuing to offer the prescribed sacrifices of animals upon God's altar, while in heart and conduct they had wandered far from Him. Under such conditions these sacrifices were no longer pleasing but distasteful to the Lord. He speaks with indignation, reminding them that He does not stand in need of the material offerings they brought: "If I were hungry, I would not tell thee: for the world is mine, and the fulness thereof," yea, "the cattle upon a thousand hills." Unless, therefore, their offerings are accompanied by genuine heart worship and thanksgiving, they might better discontinue their material sacrifices altogether.

Then as to the silver and gold mentioned by God in the book of Haggai, He has not in mind here the lavish deposits of these precious metals lying still unmined in the bowels of the earth, or distributed throughout the world. Rather is He speaking of the silver and gold in the possession of those whom

He is addressing, selfishly expended in comfortable homes and good things for themselves, or laid up in store for their future use, while they were neglecting the rebuilding of the temple of God that lay in ruins. "This people say, The time is not come, the time that the Lord's house should be built. . . . Is it time for you, O ye, to dwell in your cieled houses, and this house lie waste?" Thus does He rebuke them for withholding for their own selfish use what belongs to Him and should be used for His worship and service. He then goes on to testify how His blessing upon their crops and their labors had been withdrawn, so that they were no longer prospering but suffering need. And His exhortation follows: "Consider your ways. Go up to the mountain, and bring wood, and build the house; and I will take pleasure in it, and I will be glorified."

Surely the application of all this to God's professing people today must be altogether clear. If the silver and the gold were God's in Haggai's day, they are none the less so in our day. And if those who are His professed followers ignore this fact, deny Him His rights, and put their own selfish interests first with the money entrusted to them by Him, they need not be surprised if He withholds His blessing and bounty and allows them to suffer loss. Whether that loss be of a material or a spiritual kind, and whether it be experienced now or later, rests with God's sovereignty to decide, but that it will come in some way and at some time is certain. "Be not deceived: God is not mocked: for whatsoever a man soweth, that shall he also reap" (Gal. 6:7). Although this text is usually quoted in quite another connection, it should not be overlooked that it occurs in a passage dealing directly with the use of money. How comforting, on the other hand, are the Lord's gracious assurances through Haggai to His ancient people of His restored presence and blessing if only they will receive His rebuke and respond to His appeal! And the New Testament counterpart is Christ's admonition against anxiety over temporal needs and His accompanying promise: "But seek ye first the kingdom of God, and his righteousness; and all these things shall be added unto you." How wonderfully does "putting first things first" solve human problems as well as glorify God!

One last Old Testament passage to which we would refer is Malachi 3:8–10. The setting of this prophet's utterance was quite similar to that of Haggai's. It was a day of formalism in Israel's religious life, of outward and mechanical observance of prescribed worship, but devoid of that soul sincerity and fervor which give worship its true character. Spiritual declension characterized the people, and corruption the priests. Expressed in New Testament language, it was "a form of godliness, but denying the power thereof." The saddest and most serious thing about it was their utter unconsciousness of the fact, as evidenced by the surprised and indignant tone of their reply to the prophet's indictments. Seven times they ask the question "Wherein?" "What do you mean," they demand, "in making such charges against us? Look at our sacrifices and offerings, and our strict adherence to all the regulations laid down." What a pathetic picture it all was of contentment with the correct theory and form of worship, and even pride of orthodoxy in religion, while their actual condition was one of grievous departure from God in heart and conduct!

It is to one charge in particular brought by Malachi against these people that we would call attention, because of its direct bearing upon the subject of money. "Will a man rob God?" cries the prophet. "Yet ye rob me. But ye say, Wherein have we robbed thee? In tithes and offerings. Ye are cursed with a curse; for ye rob me, even this whole nation. Bring ye the whole tithe into the store-house, that there may be food in my house, and prove me now herewith, saith Jehovah of hosts, if I will not open you the windows of heaven, and pour you out a blessing, that there shall not be room enough to receive it."

The tithing system in ancient Israel, whereby the tenth of all one's income, whether from land or from labor, was to be offered unto the Lord, provided the means for the support of the tabernacle and priesthood. But, more than this, it was meant to teach God's people His claims upon them. The offering of the tithe was a recognition that all they possessed belonged to Him. Dr. G. Campbell Morgan in his volume on Malachi stresses the Revised Version rendering of "the whole tithe" as preferable to "all the tithes." He says that the latter words "seem to suggest a mathematical or mechanical religion, but the 'whole tithe' means not only . . . the outward form, but its inner intention. . . . 'Bring the whole tithe,' and bring it in the right way; let it come as the recognition of His love." But it would appear not only had Israel lost that true motive in their giving, but that their giving itself had fallen off as a result of spiritual backsliding. How sternly does God call them to account for this failure, bluntly charging them with robbery! This surely puts in a serious light the matter of giving of one's substance to the Lord for His service, and His people today do well to ponder it. He tells them that their unfaithfulness in this one thing was standing directly in the way of His blessing upon them, and He follows His rebuke with a touching plea, and the promise that if "the whole tithe" is brought in, He will open to them the windows of heaven and pour upon them an overflowing blessing.

Often do we hear this gracious promise quoted in prayer, and made the basis of request for an outpouring of blessing of some kind. It is indeed appropriate so to pray, if only the attached condition is observed. But the clause "prove me now *herewith*" needs to be carefully noted, and particularly that pivot word "herewith," relating distinctly as it does to the bringing in of "the whole tithe," or in other words, to fidelity to God in the stewardship of material things. Has some reader prayed earnestly for rich blessing from the Lord, perhaps for spiritual revival for himself, or for a particular church or Christian group? Then if the answer has not come, there must be some reason, for God is invariably faithful to His word. Although the reason may lie in any one of a number of things, in the instance before us here it plainly lay in withholding from ("robbing") God the material gifts that were due Him and which He expected. What a heart-searching lesson is this for every Christian—a lesson which every pastor should press home upon the consciences of his people!

Before we leave this passage there is still one other point to notice. The text says "in tithes *and offerings*." The tithe, or tenth, was not the total of Israel's gifts to Jehovah, but only the beginning. There were in addition various "offerings," some prescribed and therefore obligatory, and others voluntary and therefore optional. An estimate given by one thoughtful commentator is that the complete gifts of a devout Israelite to the service of Jehovah aggregated not merely one-tenth but more nearly three-tenths. If this proportion of his money, either demanded or expected from him, may seem to have imposed hardship, let it be remembered that the One who asked it was the "Giver of every good and perfect gift" to His people and to all His creatures, and that He was, and is, both able and disposed to provide bountifully for those whose love for Him prompts them to give liberally to Him. The faithful offerer, therefore, had no need for anxiety, but could be assured of being prospered and provided for by the Lord.

Having thus glimpsed a few of the Old Testament passages

which bear upon giving, we turn now to the fuller dealing with the subject in the New Testament. First of all let us dispose of the idea, by no means uncommonly held, that because we are now under grace and not under law the requirements laid down for those under the old dispensation have no meaning for us. This is a misconception. God is the same God now that He was then. His principles have not changed, but only His mode of dealing with His people. He works now not by the outward law of compulsion, but by the inward constraining influence of His Spirit. To quote Dr. G. Campbell Morgan once more: "Do not imagine because we are living in a spiritual dispensation we are no longer bound in the matter of material giving. We are to bring the tithes. It is not the tithe that God asks from you, but everything! You may have a proportionate statement of it if you will. As the Christian dispensation is greater than the Jewish, so must my giving be greater than a tithe, and when you have worked out the first ratio you will begin to understand the second."

God's real law of giving under grace is, "Freely ye have received, freely give" (Matt. 10:8). And yet in the New Testament giving is not left simply to the fitful impulse of the individual. Paul in writing to the Corinthian church laid down clear instructions as follows: "Now concerning the collection for the saints, as I have given order to the churches of Galatia, even so do ye. Upon the first day of the week let every one of you lay by him in store, as God hath prospered him" (I Cor. 16:1, 2). Here we see giving regarded as part of the worship of the Lord's day, along with praise and prayer, and that it is to be *voluntary* and *deliberate* ("let every one of you lay by him in store"), *systematic* ("upon the first day of the week"), and *proportionate* ("as God hath prospered him"). There is no good reason to think that this apostolic order has ceased to apply to Christians with the lapse of time. God's standards are eternal. His commands are never altered; neither can they be ignored with impunity.

Turning to the Gospels we find repeated references by Jesus to money. We read how one day He "sat over against the treasury" and watched the people casting in their offerings. If some critic may feel that to have been an unbecoming act on His part, he must reckon with Him and not with us. The fact remains that Jesus *did* so, and, we are assured, with altogether worthy motive. May He not similarly be watching and taking note as the offering plate is passed in the churches of today? We wonder whether it would make a difference in what is placed upon the plate by some if they were conscious that the Master's eye was upon them. But the important lesson in the incident is that He did not measure the gifts by their amount, but by what they cost the givers. He observed the rich as they gave out of their abundance. Presently a poor widow dropped in two mites. Then the Lord of the treasury to which the gifts were brought opened His mouth. What did He say? "This poor widow hath cast in more than they all." In so saying He was weighing the gifts not in human scales but in the balances of the sanctuary; He was estimating them not according to their intrinsic value but according to the measure of sacrifice entailed in the giving. Those gifts of the rich meant no self-denial: they cast in *"of their superfluity"* (R.V.), and thus had plenty left. The widow, on the contrary, went home penniless, having cast in *"all the living that she had."*

It was the sacrificial character of that woman's gift that Jesus prized, and this applies to all gifts and all manner of service rendered unto Him. He similarly prized the anointing of His feet by Mary of Bethany, for He well knew the personal sacrifice it must have meant to her, a humble village woman, to save enough money to purchase that pound of costly ointment with which to anoint His feet. There was also that same act of a penitent woman as Jesus sat at meat in a Pharisee's house, when the Master took occasion to contrast her deep devotion with His host's lack of common courtesy. He commended her ministry because it was prompted by love, and frankly discounted the Pharisee's hospitality because it was selfish and soulless. Thus does the Lord ever distinguish between giving that is a mere empty show or a selfish seeking of favor, and that which bears the marks of real love and sacrifice.

Jesus in His parables and discourses again and again made mention of money. The parables of the talents and the pounds deal distinctly with this subject. The parable of the rich fool sets forth the folly of hoarding this world's goods, while that of the unjust steward teaches the lesson of the use of wealth for heavenly and not for earthly aims. In the record concerning Dives and Lazarus and the prodigal son the selfish, wasteful, and sinful misuse of riches, and the grievous results that are sure to follow are searchingly pressed home. To the rich young ruler, in whom Jesus saw so many commendable traits, He put the acid test of the relation of his money to Christian discipleship. This proved too much for him, and "he went away sorrowful: for he had great possessions." How many there have been since then who while being exemplary Christians in other respects have sadly failed before this same test!

Then there is that word of the Master: "Lay not up for yourselves treasures upon earth . . . but lay up for yourselves treasures in heaven." Preachers almost invariably give a spiritual interpretation to this text, but there seems no good reason that it should not be taken literally as a frank discouraging by Jesus of selfish accumulation of money or other material wealth on the part of His followers. If He did not mean it as a stern prohibition, it was at least a word of kindly and earnest counsel by One who had their highest and most lasting interests on His heart. Laying up money down here in banks, investments and properties has unquestionably its risk of loss or deterioration. And more than this, Jesus' added words, "Where your treasure is, there will your heart be also," state—what many have learned only too late and to their sorrow—that the accumulation of treasure on earth strongly tends to draw the heart away from the things of the spiritual realm to the impoverishing of the soul. How much more profitable is the investment, and more satisfying in the end, when one gives one's money to the Lord for His work of saving precious souls and sending forth the Gospel to the ends of the earth! That truly is "laying up treasure in heaven," safe from all possibility of harm or loss, and sure of rich and eternal reward.

Perhaps the fullest treatment in the New Testament of the subject of Christian giving is that contained in II Corinthians, chapters eight and nine. As someone has expressed it, we have here "the one discourse on giving that makes needless all other treatment of this great theme." What prompted the writing of these chapters (that is, on the human side) was the splendid example of Christian benevolence furnished by the churches of Macedonia. Paul's reference to their case (8:1-5) is in language most striking, indeed paradoxical. He testifies "how that in a great trial of affliction the abundance of their joy and their deep poverty abounded unto the riches of their liberality." In this remarkable statement the giving of these believers is shown to have been a reversal of all ordinary experience. They gave out of the abundance, not of their wealth, but of their poverty; their willingness exceeded their ability, rather than vice versa. How refreshing is this testimony! The secret of it all was the grace of God operating within them. The word "grace" is mentioned six times in these two chapters which deal with giving. The fact is that *giving* is not an attribute of the natural man, whose bent is in the opposite direction of *getting* and *holding;* it is a God-given grace. That grace had been "bestowed on the churches of Macedonia," and had been received and displayed in rich measure, and that not only in the matter of their money but, what was of even greater moment, in the giving of "their own selves to the Lord" in full surrender and consecration. The Corinthian Christians are exhorted to emulate their example and to "abound in this grace also."

There is much more in these chapters bearing upon Christian giving than we have touched upon, and it is all of vital import to believers in this day. If we long for perfection in the Christian life, as every true believer should, we must realize that this grace of giving, this fruit of the Spirit, is essential to that end. Its lack is a sad blemish upon Christian character, nor can the divine blessing ever be expected to rest upon stinginess or selfishness. "God loveth a cheerful giver." He sees in him the reflection of His own love that expressed itself in "his unspeakable gift," even His beloved Son, our Saviour. And Paul here puts giving on a high plane when he states to the Corinthians that his asking for their gifts is in order *"to prove the sincerity of your love"* (8:8), and then, after mentioning the messengers whom he was sending to them he adds, "Wherefore shew ye to them, and before the churches, *the proof of your love"* (9:24). Would all Christians today be satisfied to have the sincerity of their love for Christ evaluated on the basis of their money gifts to His cause?

Still another passage that discusses the believer's attitude toward money and the bearing of this upon Christ's missionary cause is in I Timothy, chapter six. Indeed that chapter contains two passages on this subject, namely, verses six to eleven and seventeen to nineteen, and the relation of the one to the other is so impressive that we commend to our readers a careful examination of them. Reference has been made earlier to verses six and seven, and we here quote only part of verses nine to eleven. "They that are minded to be rich fall into a temptation and a snare and many foolish and hurtful lusts, such as drown men in destruction and perdition. For the love of money is a root of all kinds of evil: which some reaching after have been led astray from the faith, and have pierced themselves through with many sorrows. But thou, O man of God, flee these things. . . ." Here is an earnest admonition from the veteran missionary Paul to his junior colleague Timothy, for his own sake and also for the sake of those to whom he ministered in the Gospel.

It is a solemn warning about the deceitfulness of riches. "They that are minded to be rich" includes not only those who actually *are* rich, but those who desire or are ambitious to be so, those whose hearts are set on the accumulation of money. The phrase thus embraces many who are not in the wealthy class. We have not to look far for examples of the awful perils and tragic consequences here mentioned as attending this craving for money; they lie thick all around us. As to the sentence which immediately follows, it is one of those Scripture texts frequently misquoted. We hear people asserting that money is the root of all evil, but the text says nothing of the kind. Money in itself is intrinsically neither bad nor good. It is either bad or good only according to the use made of it. If selfishly used, or prostituted to unworthy and sinful purposes, it can indeed become "a root of all kinds of evil." It is this sad fact that has won for it the name of "filthy lucre." But over against Paul's statement here about it as such, it can be said with equal truth that the right use of money, its consecration to God and worthy ends, is "a root of all kinds of good." How thankful God's children to whom He has entrusted money, whether much or little, should be for this fact!

Now let us glance at the succeeding verses that lead up to the second passage about money in this chapter. The apostle goes on with further exhortations and charges to his beloved Timothy, and then he concludes in verses fifteen and sixteen with a beautiful ascription of praise and adoration to the Lord Jesus Christ, and ends with the benediction "to whom be honor and power eternal. Amen." It certainly seems as if this were the original close of the apostle's letter, and the absence in the Revised Version of the additional "Amen" at the end of the last verse (21) strengthens this thought. It would appear that Paul, having finished his letter, was about to dispatch it, when he was constrained to reopen it and add a further and fervent admonition. What was the subject of this important postscript? It concerned the Christian's relation to money. What he adds is partly a repetition of what he had already written, which gives his action double weight as indicating the vital importance he attached to the matter under consideration, and the burden of his heart concerning it.

Listen to the words of this postscript of his: "Charge them that are rich in this present world, that they be not high-minded, nor have their hope set on the uncertainty of riches, but on God, who giveth us richly all things to enjoy; that they do good, that they be rich in good works, that they be ready to distribute, willing to communicate; laying up in store for themselves a good foundation against the time to come, that they may lay hold on the life which is life indeed."

What an impressive word is this to God's stewards of His silver and gold! It does not say, "Congratulate them that are rich," nor yet does it say, "Envy them," or "Criticize them." All this is so easy to do, and so often done. No, it says, "*Charge* them"—be sympathetic, be faithful to them, and as a true minister of Christ seek to be helpful to them in pointing out on the one hand the danger and the responsibility of riches, and on the other hand the blessed privilege of being entrusted with money, and the unlimited possibilities of its use for the Lord's glory and the forwarding of His work of spreading the Gospel. Does not this inspired admonition lay upon pastors a sacred responsibility toward the wealthy of their flock, and upon all Christians the duty and privilege of praying for such fellow believers, that they may be given grace to be true to their trust, "that they do good, . . . be rich in good works, . . . ready to distribute, willing to communicate," and thus achieve the highest end for which riches are bestowed by God?

There is much more that the Word has to say about money, but the passages cited will serve to indicate something of its importance in the mind of God and the life of His people, and therefore its practical bearing upon the task of evangelizing the world. That missionary going depends upon missionary giving is self-evident. Through two World Wars our generation has listened to daily, at times almost hourly, appeals for bond-buying to support the gigantic military operations overseas. A familiar slogan in World War I was: "If you can't go, then give. If you can't fight in person, make your dollars fight." That states the case also for world-wide missions. Looked at from one point of view, which though admittedly not the highest one is yet a very necessary one, every missionary sent out, every field entered, every station opened, every soul won for Christ, is a matter of dollars and cents. The enterprise belongs not to the missionaries abroad but to the whole Church, and every member of that Church is charged with a share in its responsibility, and, let it be added, is favored with a share in its high privilege.

It is this aspect of privilege that we love to emphasize. The apostle Paul constantly dwelt upon it, even while so faithfully pressing home the side of responsibility. He exulted in the high honor conferred upon him of being a missionary, an ambassador of Jesus Christ. To the Ephesian church he wrote: "Unto me, who am less than the least of all saints, is this grace given, that I should preach among the Gentiles the unsearchable riches of Christ," and this is only one of several similar expressions to be found in his writings. But this high privilege is not confined to those whose part is in going. It belongs no less to those who, unable to go in person, faithfully do their part by giving. For in contributing the proceeds of their labor, by brain or by brawn, they are really giving of their very life, and the Lord accepts their offerings as such, and promises them an equal reward with those whose part is in going. This was David's way of dealing with his loyal followers. His ruling was: "As his share is that goeth down to the battle, so shall his share be that tarrieth by the stuff: they shall share alike" (I Sam. 30:24). The bountiful and cheerful givers in Philippi were told that their offerings were "an odor of a sweet smell, a sacrifice acceptable, well-pleasing to God." What a comfort and inspiration that word of commendation must have been to them, and to know that because of their monetary gifts they were reckoned the full partners of Paul and the others who were giving all their time and energy to the work of the Gospel! The same comfort and inspiration are for all Christians today who have caught the vision of the true relation of money to Christ's kingdom, and are following the example of the Macedonian believers in giving.

The need for missionary recruits is rightly stressed, but the need for missionary givers needs to be stressed no less, but perhaps even more. Instances have come under our notice where well-qualified young people have offered for foreign service only to be told that their churches were financially unprepared to send them. There is something seriously wrong and grieving to God in a situation of this kind. Where the Holy Spirit has His way, whenever He calls recruits to go, those who hold the keys to drawers in the King's treasury will as His faithful stewards be moved to release the funds to send and support them. The plea of financial inability will not hold, as is amply proven by those churches and individuals that have caught the missionary vision and risen to the task.

There is a controversy between the Lord and the devil over money as well as other things. The Lord is appealing to His people to support His missionary cause, and the devil is contriving all sorts of ways to prevent their doing so. While he tempts worldlings to squander money on things intrinsically evil, he uses other tactics with Christians, and decoys them into spending on various things which cater to pride and selfish indulgence the money that, if given to missions, would mean the saving of souls and the spiritual enriching of the givers in time and eternity.

The completion of the task of world-evangelization within the present generation is, we claim, sanely practicable through a Church that will measure up to God's conditions. But it will never be achieved without sacrifice, and that for the simple reason that God never intended it to be. He who laid the foundation of the enterprise in the sacrifice of His well-beloved Son will have it continued and finished only by sacrificial means. Sacrifice is the very soul of missions. The high cost to those who have gone to the front is clearly apparent, as expressed in arduous toil, patient endurance of suffering, and in many cases martyr death. But God has not different standards for those who go and those who stay. The latter are expected to manifest the same degree of consecration and make as great sacrifices as those who go. The red tinge of sacrifice should be upon everyone's share in this great work for Christ, wherever and whatever one's part may be. It is that which gives all service for Him its value. But after Calvary what is worthy to be called sacrifice? Can anything be deemed too costly to give to Jesus Christ?

How significant that it was on the very spot where Abraham made his supreme sacrifice of offering up Isaac, and where later David bought at full price the threshing floor of Araunah for his burnt offerings unto Jehovah, refusing to accept it as a gift and thus "offer unto the Lord of that which cost me nothing," that the glorious temple of Solomon was afterwards erected unto God! So shall the living temple of God, composed of that great multitude of souls redeemed from all nations by the precious blood shed on Calvary, be reared to completion through the sacrificial offerings of life and treasure made by the love-constrained followers of the Lamb.

IX

PRAYER AND MISSIONS

The Vital Place of Missionary Intercession

THE third factor in missions which calls for attention is prayer. While it happens that prayer comes last in the order of our present discussion, it is by no means last in importance. On the contrary, rightly conceived, prayer is the first and mightiest factor of all, inasmuch as the most vital consideration in missions is not method, or money, or even men, but it is God Himself and His mighty working, and it is ever prayer more than aught else which brings the revelation of God and calls forth His working.

But let it next be said that praying is never an acceptable substitute for going in the case of those who are qualified and able to go. In other words, going, giving, and praying are not three alternatives one of which the individual Christian may choose as his part, according to his preference. Nor will any amount of giving or praying fulfill the Great Commission to evangelize the world apart from going. The command is "Go, preach!" "Faith cometh by hearing, and hearing by the Word of God." "How shall they hear without a preacher?" But those who cannot "Go" in person can yet "Go" by prayer. Further, those who do go in person have no less the blessed privilege of sharing in the ministry of prayer, and finding in it one of the most vital and effective phases of their labor on the field.

But as it is true that praying without preaching can never carry out the missionary task, it is equally true that preaching without praying cannot do so. God has joined the two together in His Word and they are inseparable. We read in The Acts how the early apostles decided on the appointment of deacons to care for the secular affairs of the church, that they themselves might be freer for the more direct spiritual ministry, and their words were, "But we will give ourselves continually to prayer, and to the ministry of the word." Here are mentioned the two great lines of Christian ministry, prayer and preaching, and in such a way as to indicate clearly that they are coordinate and coequal. How many there are who regard preaching as being by far the more important ministry, and prayer as simply a supplementary adjunct, a kind of "aid to preaching"! But it is not so here in the Word of God. The two, prayer and preaching, are put on the same level and given the same importance; indeed, if any significance attaches to the order of the inspired words, then prayer has the precedence as being mentioned first. In point of fact, they are complementary one to the other, not two separate ministries but rather two essential parts of one ministry. Prayer is the priestly function, appearing before God in behalf of men, to plead their needs and invoke His help, while preaching is the prophetic function, appearing before men in behalf of God, to proclaim His Word of Life and implore their acceptance of it. Either one is imperfect without the other.

Missionaries are needed to go abroad and preach to the heathen, but their efforts will not reach full fruition without the support of effectual intercessors at the home end. Paul, the prince of missionaries, continually appealed to the churches for prayer. Hear his plea to the Thessalonian Christians, "Finally, brethren, pray for us, that the word of God may have free course, and be glorified." He was faithfully preaching that Word, and in the power of the Spirit, as he repeatedly claimed;

yet the fullest effect of that preaching depended upon the believing prayers of others. Again, to the Corinthian Christians he testifies to God's wonderful deliverance of him from death in Asia, but adds, "Ye also helping together by prayer for us." What a precious unity between the missionaries abroad and the churches at home do such passages express, and how inspiring to missionary-minded Christians at this end to realize that their prayers are so vital a factor in the successful labors of those who represent them on the field!

The subject of prayer is a vast one. It runs throughout the entire Scriptures. We have noted over thirty mentions of prayer in The Acts alone, an impressive indication of the place prayer was given in the early church and its missionary program. Many volumes have been written on the subject, and far from its being our purpose here to attempt any exhaustive treatment of the theme, our aim is simply to stress the vital and indispensable place of prayer in missions, by reference to a few of the many prayer passages in the Word, and of the innumerable instances of God's working through prayer in the realm of missions.

Two distinct aspects of prayer are set forth in the Word and find an essential place in the life of all true missionaries, and indeed of all spiritually minded Christians. They are respectively the devotional and the intercessory aspects.

1. Devotional Prayer. This is communion with God, a holy, intimate and growing fellowship, cultivated by regular seasons of waiting upon Him in adoring worship and quiet meditation on His Word. The book of Psalms abounds in passages illustrating this aspect of prayer, while its supreme example is the Lord Jesus Himself, whose communion with the Father throughout His life on earth was unbroken and intensely real. Jesus was a man of prayer, or more correctly, THE Man

of prayer. His life began, continued, and ended in prayer. Limited as is the record given of His earthly career, it includes impressive glimpses into His prayer life. We see Him praying at His baptism, in His wilderness temptation, on the mount of transfiguration, at the grave of Lazarus, in the garden of Gethsemane, on the Cross of Calvary. He prayed in public and in private. He spent whole nights alone in prayer, one of these before choosing the twelve apostles. After a typically strenuous Sabbath day's ministry in Capernaum, as described in Mark's first chapter, the next morning "rising up a great while before day, he went out, and departed into a solitary place, and there prayed." Jesus could not live without regular communion with His Father. To Him it was essential for the daily sustaining of His spiritual life, the replenishing of His spiritual power so lavishly spent in ministry to others. He could do without food, without sleep, without everything except prayer. *That* He must have at any cost, since it was the channel of constant fellowship with the Father, upon whom He depended absolutely for all that pertained to His life and service down here. Testimony as to this fact is found in His own words such as these: "I live by the Father." "The Son can do nothing of himself, but what he seeth the Father do." "I can of mine own self do nothing." "The words that I speak unto you I speak not of myself."

Now if the very Son of God felt such utter need of daily devotional prayer, what presumption it is on the part of any human missionary or other Christian worker to attempt to do without it! The words of I John 2:6 apply searchingly in this connection: "He that saith he abideth in him ought himself also so to walk, even as he walked." Yes, prayer is the essential preparation for Christian service, for it is through secret touch and communion with the Lord that He unveils, reveals, and imparts Himself, and that the life of the Vine flows freely through the branches and enables them to bear fruit (Jno. 15:4, 5). Without doubt much of the shallowness of Christian experience and the feebleness of Christian service is to be traced to the poverty of the prayer life.

The men who have accomplished most for God have been men of prayer. John Wesley was wont to spend at least two hours each day in prayer. Samuel Rutherford rose at three o'clock each morning to wait upon God. John Fletcher was said to have stained the walls of his chamber by the breath of his prayers. The greatest missionaries have been uniformly men of prayer. The names of David Brainerd and Henry Martyn stand out as among the brightest stars in the missionary firmament because of the profound influence they exerted upon their own and every succeeding generation. But this influence was due primarily not to their active labors, for they died at the early ages of twenty-nine and thirty-one respectively. Rather was it due to the depth of their prayer life and the resultant saintly character that it produced in them. And who can fully measure the effect upon thousands of souls in India and throughout the world of the unique prayer life of "Praying Hyde"?

Adoniram Judson, one of the greatest of America's missionary sons, was emphatic in his insistence upon prayer. Wrote he: "Be resolute in prayer. Make any sacrifice to maintain it. Consider that time is short and that business and company must not be allowed to rob thee of thy God." That was the man who mightily impressed a great empire for Christ and laid deep and strong the foundations of God's kingdom in Burma. Hudson Taylor was before all else a man of prayer. He lived in the conscious presence of the Lord, constant communion with Whom had become to him as necessary and natural as breathing. The China Inland Mission, which he founded, was born in prayer, and prayer has ever since been its vital breath.

The list of men who have found in prayer the secret of their own highest blessing and of their power in service could be extended indefinitely. But those mentioned must suffice to illustrate and emphasize both the absolute need and the blessed result of the habitual practice of devotional prayer by those who would be the Lord's true missionaries, whether on the foreign field or at home. To quote from that heart-searching little volume *Preacher and Prayer* by E. M. Bounds: "What the Church needs today is not more machinery or better, not new organizations or more and novel methods, but men whom the Holy Ghost can use—men of prayer, men mighty in prayer. The Holy Ghost does not flow through methods, but through men. He does not come on machinery, but on men. He does not anoint plans, but men—men of prayer."

The maintenance of regular daily seasons of devotional prayer (together with Bible meditation) by the missionary on the field will not be found easy. Lack of privacy in makeshift places of abode, incessant interruptions by well-meaning but undiscerning persons, pressure of manifold duties, the oppressive atmosphere of surrounding heathenism—all these are detracting and distracting forces to be met. And yet the paramount importance of safeguarding and nourishing by this essential means the missionary's spiritual life, upon which his sustained victory, Christlike influence, and effective service absolutely depend, makes it imperative that he allow nothing to interfere with fixed and frequent trysting times with his Lord.

2. Intercessory Prayer. This is quite different from devotional prayer. The latter is very real and precious, and its vital importance has already been stressed. But it needs to be

remembered that prayer is not merely communion with God; it is also cooperation with God, a definite and aggressive ministry, a partnership with God in the carrying out of His divine will and purposes in the world. Prayer is thus more than simply preparation for service; it is power in service—yes, even more than that, prayer IS service.

Among the many Bible passages setting forth this aspect of prayer, one to which we would specially call attention is the last clause of James 5:16. Neither the King James Version nor yet the American Revision gives the full force of the original, and we venture here to give the English equivalent of the translation as it appears in the latest Chinese edition of the New Testament, which is highly commendable for its accuracy. The text would thus read: "The energy put forth by the fervent prayer of a righteous man issues in mighty results," or "brings mighty things to pass." This rendering has the merit of emphasizing the truth that prayer is a vital force, a great dynamic, that prayer exerts energy, and brings things to pass outside the one who prays.

We are aware that some individuals will object to this conception of prayer, their contention being that since the universe is governed by certain fixed and unalterable laws, it is therefore unthinkable that any mere man, by his praying, should be able to interfere with such fixed laws. But these objectors lose sight of the important fact that prayer itself IS one of these fixed laws of God, and that God has designed to bring many things to pass by means of prayer. When that fact is recognized, it will at once be seen that it is not the man who prays, but rather the man who does *not* pray, who interferes with God's fixed laws, by failing to cooperate with God in bringing about things which He has meant to be accomplished through His law of prayer.

An illustration which should help to clarify this point is the force of electricity. Is electricity something that did not exist until the last generation or two? Or will anyone claim that there is more electricity in the world today than a century ago? Yet how amazed and incredulous would our great-grand-parents be if they could behold the multiplied forms of applied electricity in daily operation today. We drive our vehicles and trains, light and heat our homes, cook our food, wash our clothes, and do all manner of other things by electricity. Are we then to conclude that the men of the present generation have violated some law of nature in bringing about these new and strange things? By no means! They have simply dis-covered a latent force, always in existence but not under-stood and utilized, and by discovering and harnessing this force they have achieved mighty things undreamed of by earlier generations.

Similarly, prayer is a mighty spiritual dynamic, but which has been largely hidden, undiscovered, a buried talent, an un-known power. Yet certain saints who have lived close enough to God have come to apprehend this secret, with the result that by laying hold upon its mystic power they have been en-abled to achieve results unthought of by others.

If any further proof is needed to support the claim that prayer brings things to pass outside the one who prays, that "Prayer Changes Things," as the familiar motto puts it, then the incident cited immediately following this text in James' epistle supplies that proof. It is the story of Elijah as told in I Kings. First, for our encouragement we are told that Elijah was "a man subject to like passions as we are," that is to say, he was no prodigy or superman, but simply a person of flesh and blood like ourselves, without special powers inherent in himself, or any resources such as we have not. Then follows the account of his meeting with Ahab, and his announcement of an impending drought as a punishment from God upon that wicked king and nation because of their sin.

But the statement in James goes beyond the Old Testament narrative in affirming that that drought of three and a half years, and likewise the rain which followed it, were not merely foretold by Elijah but were actually *brought about by his praying*: "Elijah prayed, and it rained not . . . and he prayed again, and the heaven gave rain." Here, then, is an instance of a man so in tune with God that he could catch God's thought, turn that thought into prayer, and thus become the means God used for the working out of His divine purpose.

Nor is this case to be regarded as an exception to the rule of God's working, for other instances of the kind are to be found all through the Word. We recall Abraham as he pleaded for Sodom, Moses as he agonized in the mount for gainsaying Israel, Daniel as he prostrated himself by the riverside supplicating for his captive race, and Nehemiah as he persistently interceded for his people and moved the heart of a heathen monarch to decree and sponsor the rebuilding of the Holy City, and brought to nought the crafty devices of Israel's enemies to obstruct the project. All these are similar illustrations of the impressive truth that God chooses to use prayer as one of His ordained means for the accomplishment of His plans and purposes in the world.

A further point to be noted regarding these instances of intercession is that they did not concern merely small affairs of a personal or local nature. In every case it was community, or national, or even international issues of vast import that were involved. Yet these men were not listed among the recognized statesmen of their times: they were but humble, behind-the-scenes men, two of them indeed captives in foreign countries, and another a peasant living in obscurity. But they were statesmen at the high court of heaven, mighty men of prayer, and God who rules supreme over all the affairs of men and nations gave heed to their cries, and actually made their intercessions the pivot upon which momentous national and world issues turned. In very truth, their prayers "put forth energy," and "issued in mighty results," or "brought mighty things to pass."

In no other realm have the primacy and the power of prayer been so overwhelmingly demonstrated as in the realm of missions. We speak of Pentecost as being the starting point or inauguration day of Christian missions. But we must not forget that the upper room in Jerusalem where that devout company of disciples "continued with one accord in prayer and supplication" for ten days was the necessary preparation, on the human side, for Pentecost, so that the beginning of missions can consistently be dated from that prayer gathering. The missionary enterprise was born in prayer, and its entire subsequent history has been a record of answered prayer.

The Acts is a great textbook on prayer. Prayer permeated the life of the Church of that period, and saturated its plans and activities. Two instances, recorded in chapters four and twelve, are positively dramatic. One was the prayer meeting held upon the release of the two of the apostles from arrest for preaching in Jerusalem, with a threat of severer punishment if the offense were repeated. The prayer that company offered is no less striking for what it *did not* ask than for what it *did* ask. It pleaded not for revenge, or vindication, or exemption from further persecution, but for grace to endure and courage to continue at any cost, and for God's mighty power to attend their efforts. What was the result? "The place was shaken where they were assembled together; and they were all filled with the Holy Ghost, and they spake the word of God with boldness . . . And with great power gave the apostles witness of the resurrection of the Lord Jesus: and great grace was upon them all." The other occasion was the imprisonment of Peter and his impending execution. The extremely critical situation having been described, the statement then follows: "*but prayer* was made without ceasing of the church unto God for him." Thereupon came God's miraculous deliverance of His servant and his sudden arrival at the home of Mary, "where many were gathered together praying." Still another impressive passage, in chapter thirteen, pictures the godly leaders of the Antioch church as they waited upon the Lord, received His direct guidance as to the choice of two to go from their midst as missionaries, and then—"when they had fasted and prayed, and laid their hands on them, they sent them away." But these are only high spots in a continuous succession of answers to prayer of which The Acts consists. Truly, in the words of Neesima of Japan, the early church "advanced upon its knees."

Paul, the greatest of all human missionaries, was at his very best in prayer. From the first hour of his new life in Christ, when the word conveyed to Ananias concerning him was, "Behold, he prayeth," he lived and moved in the realm of prayer. Any worthy consideration of his recorded prayers would require a whole volume. Our present aim being to point out the bearing of prayer upon missions, we shall refer to only two Pauline texts as illustrating this truth. One of these texts occurs in that great passage, Ephesians 6:10–20, which describes the Christian warfare. While many persons interpret these verses as applying to the Christian's defensive warfare against his spiritual foes, we have long held that they reach their fullest meaning only when applied to the great offensive warfare waged by the Christian soldier against the mighty hosts of Satan which hotly oppose the progress of Christ's cause.

In other words, this passage sets forth the missionary conflict in its true and solemn significance. The fight is not merely against "flesh and blood," or the ignorance, superstition, racial antipathy, and the like, of the heathen; but against "the principalities, the powers, the world-rulers of this darkness, the spiritual hosts of wickedness in the heavenlies." That is to say, the real foe is a highly organized, powerful, and desperately tenacious host of wicked spirits, controlled and directed by the devil himself, arrayed against Christ's Gospel messengers in their penetration of areas over which these evil spirits have so long held undisputed sway. The missionary must not underrate the strength of the enemy he faces, but is admonished to "put on the whole armor of God" as his only hope of "withstanding in the evil day, and having done all, to stand." This armor is then described in detail—the girdle, breastplate, shoes, shield, helmet, and sword. The spiritual significance of each of these parts of the armor has become familiar through frequent exposition of the passage. But a point which calls for more attention than has usually been given it is that this whole order of Christian armor leads up to, and climaxes in, the weapon of "all-prayer." Moffatt renders the verse thus: "Praying at all times in the Spirit with all manner of prayer and entreaty—be alive to that, attend to it unceasingly, interceding on behalf of all the saints and on my [Paul the missionary's] behalf also, that I may be allowed to speak and open my lips in order to expound fully and freely that open secret of the gospel for the sake of which I am in custody as its envoy. Pray that I may have freedom to declare it as I should."

What a tremendous plea for missionary intercession is in

these pungent words of the great apostle, words born of his own conviction and experience that prayer, the kind of prayer here spoken of, is the mightiest weapon man can wield for the defeat of these satanic powers, and the triumph of the Gospel in heathen lands! If it were simply a matter of facing the false ideas, prejudices, or hostility of "flesh and blood" human beings, the missionary might hope that friendly approach, sound argument, and tactful persuasion could meet the case. But to encounter the invisible but terribly real and malicious spirit forces behind these human beings, forces which blind their minds, harden their hearts, and hold them in a deadly grip— that is a vastly different thing. Such opposing forces can be met and overcome only by this spiritual weapon of "all-prayer" that boldly approaches the throne of God and calls forth "the working of his mighty power" against these wicked adversaries. Thank God, that weapon is a part of "the whole armor of God" provided for the soldier of the Cross and made available to him through appropriating faith. Although in himself he is no match for the devil, yet like Michael the archangel (as recorded in Jude) he can say in faith, "The Lord rebuke thee," and it shall be done.

The other prayer passage in Paul's writings to which we would call attention is Romans 15:30–32: "Now I beseech you, brethren, . . . that ye strive together with me in your prayers to God for me; that I may be delivered from them that do not believe in Judaea; and that my service which I have for Jerusalem may be accepted of the saints; that I may come unto you with joy by the will of God, and may with you be refreshed." This is a most impressive passage. It presents two thoughts: (1) the *manner* and (2) the *matter* of Paul's own prayer and of the supporting prayers of those to whom he wrote. As to the *manner*, the word "strive" here used is literally our word "agonize," and is much the strongest of the several words used in the New Testament to express prayer. Only in two other instances is it used in this connection, namely, in Colossians 4:12, where Epaphras is spoken of as "always laboring fervently [lit. agonizing] in prayer" for the Colossian church, and in Luke 22:44 (in its noun form) of our blessed Lord, where it is recorded that "being in an agony he prayed more earnestly." The expression serves to emphasize the intense nature of true missionary intercession. It is no easy thing, but strenuous labor, travail of soul, that takes a heavy toll of one's strength. To quote Hudson Taylor: "If we are simply to pray to the extent of a pleasant exercise, and know nothing of watching and weariness in prayer, we shall not draw down the blessing that we might. We shall not sustain our missionaries who are overwhelmed with the appalling darkness of heathenism. It is ever true that what costs little is worth little." Then as to the *matter* of this prayer request of Paul, three specific objects are to be noted—his deliverance from enemies in Judaea, the acceptance of his ministry to the Jerusalem saints, and his reaching Rome in safety and with joy. Now the reading of chapters twenty-one through twenty-seven of The Acts as a commentary upon these three prayer requests will prove a spiritual tonic indeed, as the complete answers to all three of them are traced, and through a maze of desperate efforts by Satan to defeat them.

From Pentecost and the apostle Paul right down through the centuries to the present day, the story of missions has been the story of answered prayer. Every fresh outbreak of missionary energy has been the result of believing prayer. Every new missionary undertaking that has been owned and blessed of God has been the germinating of seed planted by the divine Spirit in the hearts of praying saints.

Organized missionary enterprise began in Germany and Denmark a century earlier than in England. It sprang directly from the revival movement known as Pietism, under the godly leadership of Spener and Francke and deeply rooted in prayer. Out of it came the Danish-Halle Mission to India, and also the better known Moravian movement led by saintly Count Zinzendorf. A settlement was founded at Herrnhut ("The Lord's Watch"), which became the center of the Moravian Brotherhood, and where a life of prayer developed such an effusion of missionary zeal as has made that little community, and the long line of devoted missionaries who have gone forth from it to the ends of the earth, one of the wonders of the Church age.

Herrnhut in turn exerted a distinct influence upon the great leaders of Methodism in England, where early in the eighteenth century a marked revival of prayer for the heathen world broke out, greatly stimulated also by a powerful appeal issued by Robert Millar of Scotland urging prayer as foremost among the measures for the conversion of the heathen. In 1744 a call was widely circulated for a sustained concert of prayer, and in 1746 a memorial was sent to America inviting all Christians there to unite in the same petition. This message moved Jonathan Edwards to preach a sermon which not only awakened many on this side of the Atlantic to more earnest prayer, but which also proved to be one of the influences that stirred the heart of William Carey in England, and thus contributed to initiating the modern period of missions.

The facts pertaining to the beginnings of this new era of missions are too well known to need repeating. Nor is it our present object to dwell upon the record itself but simply upon the vital factor of prayer in bringing it about. As related to Great Britain, William Carey is universally recognized as "The Father of Modern Missions," and the same title is justly due

Samuel J. Mills as related to North America. One cannot read the story of either one without being profoundly stirred. Kettering in England, where the first Baptist Missionary Society was founded in 1792, and the "Haystack prayer meeting" of 1806 at Williams College in the USA will always be spoken of as the birthplaces of modern missions. But it was in the hearts of Carey and Mills, and through their travail of soul and strong wrestling in prayer, that this great enterprise for Christ and the world was actually born. Just as truly can it be said that the China Inland Mission and the Gossner Mission in India, two notable "Faith Missions," were born in the hearts and through the agonizing prayers of their respective founders, Hudson Taylor of England and Pastor Gossner of Germany. The prayer life of the former of these has already been mentioned. Of Gossner, who single-handed sent out 144 missionaries, it was said: "He prayed up the walls of a hospital, and the hearts of the nurses; he prayed mission stations into being, and missionaries into faith. . . . Prayer was his atmosphere: he could not live without it."

All the mighty spiritual revivals which constitute the mountain peaks of missionary annals had their roots in prayer. The one in Hawaii known as "The Great Awakening," which continued from 1837 to 1843, began in the hearts of the missionaries themselves. As they assembled for their annual meetings in 1835 and 1836, involving for some of them six weeks of weary travel in crude and filthy boats, "they were powerfully moved to pray, and were so deeply impressed with the need of an outpouring of the Spirit that they prepared a strong appeal to the home churches urging Christians everywhere to unite with them in prayer for a baptism from on high." Soon they saw unmistakable signs of deepening interest in spiritual things. Then, in 1837, a revival swept the island, so that missionaries labored day and night with throngs of anxious souls. On one memorable day at Hilo, 1,705 were baptized by Titus Coan, and within six years 27,000 converts were received into the church.

The story of the great revival among the Telugu outcastes of India is vitally linked with "Prayer-meeting Hill," a high hill overlooking the town of Ongole. A missionary couple and three like-minded Hindu helpers on a preaching tour were constrained to spend the last night of 1853 on that hilltop in prayer for the Telugu field, which after many years of faithful toil had yielded almost no fruit. More than once the Board at home had been on the point of abandoning it, and only upon the earnest plea of the missionaries had this action been postponed. Just as the first day of the new year began to dawn, a sweet sense of assurance that their prayers had prevailed stole into their hearts. A further long period of testing had still to be faced, but gradually the opposition broke, the tide began to turn, and finally a mighty outpouring of the Spirit brought a multitude of souls into the kingdom. In a single day at Ongole, in 1878, 2,222 were baptized, and 8,000 within six weeks, and the church there became the largest in the world. An added note of interest is that "the Government of India has acknowledged the power emanating from Prayer-meeting Hill by donating the hilltop to the Mission to be used as a memorial and gathering place."

Perhaps the greatest of all revivals on the mission field was that in Korea during 1905–1907, when one of the most remarkable manifestations of God's power in the entire history of the Christian Church took place. It swept over the whole land and across its borders into Manchuria and China. It cleansed and purified the church, bringing an overwhelming realization of the awfulness of sin. It fired the Christians with a new passion to seek the lost, great numbers of whom were smitten with pungent conviction and led to accept Christ. It prepared the way for the "Million Souls Movement" which was vigorously carried on for years. Like all other revivals this one began with prayer, first by a group of workers in eastern Korea, where the earlier stirring was felt, and later in Pyeng Yang in the west, which became the center of "The Great Revival." For months previous to this awakening the missionaries of that station had held daily prayer meetings pleading for a mighty outpouring of God's Spirit. Finally the flood of blessing broke upon a large assembly of Korean workers and believers gathered for prayer in the great Central Church of the city, led by a humble but godly Korean evangelist.

A sequel to the Korean revival was an extended series of much blessed revival services in China conducted by Dr. Jonathan Goforth, who had visited Korea and seen the mighty working of the Lord there. As touching the prayer factor in this revival movement, the following impressive testimony was later given by Dr. Goforth: "When I came to England I met a certain saint of God. We talked about the revival in China, and she gave me certain dates when God specially pressed her to pray. I was almost startled on looking up these dates to find that they were the very dates when God was doing His mightiest work in Manchuria and China. . . . I believe the day will come when the whole inward history of that revival will be unveiled, and will show that it was not the one who speaks to you now, but some of God's saints hidden away with Him in prayer who did most to bring it about."

Other thrilling instances of the Spirit's mighty working in a great variety of ways as a direct result of prayer are far too many to enumerate. There lie before us at this moment half a dozen volumes packed full of similar records on different mission fields. China Inland Mission history alone furnishes a wealth of wonderful instances of answered prayer. Take, for example, the Appeal for Seventy new missionaries, conceived in a prayer conference of Mr. Taylor and a dozen fellow workers in 1880, when the Mission's total staff as yet numbered only about one hundred. After days of united waiting on God, all hearts were filled with such assurance that before the party scattered they held a praise meeting to give thanks for The Seventy *received by faith.* Then followed the Appeal for One Hundred to be sent out in 1887, issued after protracted prayer by the entire membership of the Mission on the field. So confident was Mr. Taylor that God had heard and answered that he remarked: "If you showed me a photograph of the whole hundred, taken in China, I could not be more sure than I am now." In both cases the full number asked for reached China within the specified time, all the money for outfits and passages having been supplied. And, perhaps most wonderful of all, Mr. Taylor's special prayer in the case of the One Hundred that the Lord might be pleased to send in the needed funds in a few large amounts, to obviate extra work on the part of the hard-pressed office staff, was so literally answered that the required £11,000 was received in just *eleven gifts.*

But these are only a sample of hundreds of answers to prayer in this one Mission and field, and in many others as well, in the form not merely of financial supplies, but of signal deliverances from danger and death, physical healing, divine intervention in famine, flood, pestilence, riots, plots and attacks by hostile natives, and other contingencies of every conceivable kind. For further research on this subject which will yield great spiritual enrichment to any who will pursue it, we would suggest the experiences of John G. Paton and his fellow workers in the

New Hebrides, Livingstone and Moffat in Africa, Gardiner and Grubb in South America, Hans Egede and Grenfell in the Far North, among many others. Equally noteworthy are the wonderful answers to prayer and manifestations of divine power and blessing in the lives and ministries of native workers such as Pandita Ramabai and Sadhu Sundar Singh of India, Pastor Hsi and Ting Li Mei of China, Neesima of Japan, and a host of others who although less well known in the West have similarly learned the secret of prevailing prayer. "One of the greatest miracles and pieces of evidence of Christianity is the prayer life of Oriental Christians, newly won to Christ. In all these multitudes of India, China, Japan, Africa, and the Islands of the Sea we find the same phenomenon—*they pray*." This testimony of a leading writer on missions finds impressive illustration in the frequent whole days of prayer and fasting observed by large companies of Chinese Christians during the years of their nation's sufferings from Japanese invasion and warfare. The spiritual atmosphere of these gatherings and the fervent prayers offered have been reminiscent of the days of The Acts.

If all that has thus been said about the power and the achievements of prayer is true, then is it not a fresh challenge to every Christian to embrace this sublimest privilege of cooperating with God by prayer, which more than aught else releases His mighty power? We say *"every* Christian" advisedly, for missionary praying, unlike going, or giving, is something in which every child of God can have a part. *All* cannot go, for going calls for special qualifications and training. *All* cannot give, at least in liberal amount, because of limited resources. But *all* can pray. The humblest Christian, who may have no public gift or talent, the illiterate, and even the shut-in and bed-ridden one, can share this highest and mightiest ministry of intercession. Indeed some of the greatest missionary intercessors have been among these last mentioned, who have turned their bed chambers into audience rooms with the King, and by way of the throne of grace have projected themselves far beyond the range of any preacher, and touched and influenced the very uttermost parts of the earth for Christ.

Fervently do we thank God for all faithful intercessors and their prayers. They have been God's means of breaking down barriers, turning the hearts of kings and rulers, forcing open closed doors, calling forth workers, releasing money to support them, giving impelling power to preaching, softening hard hearts and bringing them under conviction, turning threatened defeat into victory in the hour of crisis—all this and much besides. But the need is for a multitude more of such intercessors, yea, for the whole Church to be driven to its knees under a burden of deep concern and a quickened sense of responsibility. One book on this subject bears the title, "GOD'S DYNAMITE; Changing a World by Prayer." Its Introduction says: "Prayer is a high explosive. It rends the rocks in pieces, but it also liberates great constructive energies." But it adds: "The greatest problem of foreign missions lies in the home land. . . . Will the spiritual life of the churches at home develop in such fashion as to support the weight of the great structure abroad? . . . The answer is found in prayer—prayer which will lead to service and sacrifice."

The following quotations from other sources are no less pertinent, and heart-searching as well:

When the Church sets itself to pray with the same seriousness and strength of purpose that it has devoted to other forms of Christian effort, it will see the Kingdom of God come with power.
—Report of Edinburgh Missionary Conference.

When the prayer-life of the people of God comes to be the dominant feature of Christian experience, the power of God will sweep the earth with the victories of grace.

—Howard Agnew Johnston.

The prayer power has never been tried to its full capacity in any church. If we want to see mighty wonders of divine grace and power wrought in the place of weakness, failure and disappointment, let the whole Church answer God's standing challenge: "Call unto me, and I will answer thee, and show thee great and mighty things, which thou knowest not."

—J. Hudson Taylor.

Indelibly imprinted upon our memory are words of Dr. A. C. Dixon in a sermon preached years ago. They ran something like this: "When we rely upon organization, we get what organization can do; when we rely upon education, we get what education can do; when we rely upon eloquence, we get what eloquence can do. And so on. But when we rely upon prayer, *we get what God can do*." Surely that is what is needed above all else—what God can do. And, we believe, that is what many of God's people earnestly desire. Then that need, that desire, will become an actual and a glorious experience when prayer is given its rightful place in Christian life and missionary service. *"Lord, teach us to PRAY."*

X

THE "LITTLE LAD" * AND MISSIONS

The Feeding of the Multitude—a Missionary Parable

IN OUR opening chapter the missionary character of the teachings and ministry of Jesus as set forth in the four Gospels was mentioned. In this closing chapter we propose to consider one particular miracle of Jesus as constituting a unique and striking illustration of some of the fundamental principles of missions. That miracle is the feeding of the five thousand.

The importance which the Holy Spirit, who inspired the writing of the Scriptures, attaches to this miracle is indicated by His choosing to give us four versions of it, one in each of the four Gospels. This is true of no other of our Saviour's miracles, and indeed of very few incidents in His entire life. For example, we have not four records of Christ's birth, or of His baptism, temptation, transfiguration, or ascension, or of a single one of His parables, prayers, or discourses. Of a few events we do have four records, namely, His agony in the garden, His trial and condemnation, His death, burial, and resurrection, and finally His Great Commission.

Is it not impressive that along with these great outstanding events, which are recognized as constituting the very foundation truths of the Christian faith, four records have also been given of this particular miracle? The repetition surely cannot be without significance, and we believe the reason is that this incident is more than simply one among many miracles: it is

---

* The Greek word *paidarion* used in John 6:9 is the diminutive of *pais* and is accurately translated "little lad."

a parable as well. A parable of what? someone asks. A parable
of missions, we reply. We believe that when Jesus broke that
material bread to appease the physical hunger of the multitude
on the shore of Galilee that evening, He had in His vision the
infinitely larger multitude of men and women the world over
and the centuries across, starving not for material food but for
the Bread of Life, and that He wrought that miracle not
merely to satisfy the physical hunger of those before Him, but
also to unfold to His disciples, then and ever since, the divine
principle and method of giving the Gospel of salvation to
earth's perishing millions. For this reason we choose to regard
this incident as a parable, a parabolic miracle, if you will.

The incident furnishes much rich teaching into which we
cannot here enter, but keeping the missionary application in
mind we would direct attention to three statements made about
Jesus, and the thoughts which these utterances suggest. It is
said of Him first, that He *saw;* next, that He *felt;* and finally,
that He *acted.* That He saw suggests *vision;* that He felt suggests *compassion;* and that He acted suggests *consecration.*
Three great missionary lessons thus stand out boldly in this
missionary parable: (1) the need of vision, (2) the need of
compassion, (3) the need of consecrated action.

THE NEED OF VISION

The thought of vision runs all through the Bible. To Abraham God gave the vision of the promised land, saying to him:
"Lift up now thine eyes, and look, . . . For all the land which
thou seest, to thee will I give it, and to thy seed forever." This
was a call to discern and appropriate divinely proffered blessings. To Job, to Isaiah, and to John on Patmos the Lord gave
the exalted vision of Himself, with profound spiritual results
to each of them. But the passage before us speaks of the vision

of the needy multitude. "When Jesus then *lifted up his eyes*," He saw a great throng of hungry people. In this, alas, He stood out in contrast to His disciples, for they did not lift up their eyes, and hence did not share His vision. Do we not see all too accurately mirrored in these disciples a large proportion of Christ's professed followers today?

In the first place, theirs was a selfish vision. They had just finished a campaign afield and had come with Jesus to a quiet place for rest and fellowship, when their privacy was suddenly broken in upon by a rude mob of inquisitive people. They quite evidently resented the intrusion. They would much rather have been left to enjoy their Master by themselves. How much has selfishness been responsible for the failure of the Church all through its history to carry out her Lord's Commission! There is *personal* selfishness, that considers only its own comfort, ease, and indulgence, and has never "lifted up the eyes" to behold others' needs. There is *religious* selfishness, represented in costly church edifices, rich adornment, elaborate ritual, fine music and floral decorations, or again in denominational ambition which insists upon planting several churches, each with a mere handful of attendants, and many of them struggling to meet expenses, in small communities where one church would amply suffice. There is *spiritual* selfishness, if we may so speak, which prides itself on knowing Scripture truth better than others do, and glories in an orthodoxy that is cold and dead, wrapping about itself the robes of self-complacency, but never stooping to extend a helping hand to fallen and needy sinners. It is even possible for Bible conferences to become selfish, when they are devoid of any altruistic outlook along evangelistic or missionary lines.

Again, theirs was a prejudiced vision. It was the same group that Jesus led one day into Samaria, away from their own province, from their kith and kin, and bade them lift up their eyes *there* and behold a harvest field for missionary effort, among those mongrel Samaritans whom they as Jews looked upon with contempt. How that prejudiced vision has persisted ever since in the favored lands of the West, and even among professing Christians, revealing itself in pride of so many kinds —pride of race, of learning, of privilege, of wealth, of power, and much else! We Anglo-Saxons find it especially hard to divest ourselves entirely of the deeply imbedded notion that we are superior to other races, and are made of altogether better stuff than the Orientals. Kipling's lines, "Yet East is East, and West is West, and never the twain shall meet," are quoted as if they were a part of Holy Writ. They carry the implication, of course, of an immense superiority of Occidentals over Orientals, but further, that the differences between the two constitute a wide gulf which can never be bridged. The fallacy of this claim is exposed by the Word, which states that "God hath made of one blood all nations for to dwell on the face of the earth," and the unity and solidarity of the human race as thus stated is confirmed by every honest and thoughtful world traveler. While differences of physiognomy, speech, dress, customs, and mode of living are to be observed, these are all superficial, and when you get under the skin you find that all men are fundamentally alike. They all love and hate. They all know joy and sorrow. Above all, they all sin, and therefore all need the same Saviour.

As to the Westerner's smug feeling of superiority, it would be well for him to dip back into the earlier centuries and note the condition of his "Occidental" forbears in Europe before the Gospel was first brought to that continent by "Oriental" missionaries from Asia, and to remember that Christianity originated in that continent, not in Europe, much less in Amer-

ica. No, any superiority we may boast over the peoples of the
East is not inherent in us, but is to be attributed to the uplifting
influences and the great advantages of every kind which the
Gospel has brought to us. But had that "man of Macedonia"
whom Paul saw in his vision been a man of India, China, or
some other Eastern land, and in the providence of God Christianity had spread eastward over Asia instead of westward
over Europe, then the tables would be turned, with the result
that we would be today sitting in heathen darkness and degradation, while they would be basking in the light and warmth
of the Gospel with its manifold blessings. There is, moreover,
abundant missionary testimony to the fact that in many cases
converts from those heathen lands far surpass the average
Western Christian in their spiritual development, and in their
devoted and effective service for God and their fellow men.
We then do well to recognize with Paul that only "by the
grace of God I am what I am," and to see to it that we are
doing as much for their uplift and salvation as we would hope
that they would do for ours if the situation were reversed.

Furthermore, theirs was a distorted vision. They imagined
that God's interest and His purposes began and ended in the
Jew, to the utter ignoring of the Gentile. But have not many
Westerners much of the same distorted vision of their own
nation as compared with others? It is by no means uncommon
to hear church members protest against the sending of our
fine young men and women to heathen countries, on the plea
that "we need them at home," that "we should convert America first," and the like. What an utter misconception of the
mind and plan of Him who said, "God so loved *the world*,"
"The field is *the world*," "Go ye into *all the world*, and preach
the gospel to *every creature*"!

But such a distorted vision is not merely wrong: it is absolutely futile and hopeless as well. What has it accomplished in line with its own proposals? Has Christianity in America or any other enlightened country been prospered and bettered by the policy of concentrating upon itself and withholding the light of the Gospel from other lands that need it, and need it so desperately? Has any one of these enlightened countries been "converted" in the true evangelical sense of that word, or has substantial progress been made toward such a goal? The only honest answer is "No," and the sad fact is that the trend has been in the opposite direction. Light given by God but not walked in, and not shared with others, becomes darkness. "If the light that is in thee," said Jesus, "be darkness, how great is that darkness!" That "there is still work to do at home," as those with a distorted and selfish vision keep saying, is true enough. And, let it be added, there will be more and yet more work to do at home so long as the program set by Christ's Great Commission is ignored or treated indifferently. Furthermore, it is work that might never have needed to be done had the Church more faithfully followed her explicit marching orders.

The story of the children of Israel and God's dealings with them furnishes many a pointed lesson for the Church today, and one incident seems to fit the case we are now discussing. When they gathered manna in the wilderness, there were some among them who hoarded the manna selfishly, with the result that it bred worms and stank. It is not a pleasant comparison to draw, but it is our belief that the Higher Criticism and rank Modernism that have swept like a flood into the Church of to-day, working distressing mischief, are nothing else than the worms that have been bred in the hoarded manna of the Gospel. If the Church had kept going afield as it was told to do, and had distributed more faithfully the Gospel manna to the hungry and neglected multitudes of other lands, it would have been kept sweet and wholesome, and free from heresies and vagaries. It would not have bred these worms, and would have been spared the distressing harm and loss they have brought upon it.

This last thought leads on to the interesting question as to just when and how those loaves and fishes were multiplied to feed "five thousand men, beside women and children." Our own conviction is that they were not multiplied while still in Jesus' hands, for obviously He could not have held any such amount of food at one time. For the same obvious reason the miracle of multiplication could not have taken place while the loaves remained in the hands of the twelve disciples. We believe it occurred in the very instant and act of the giving away by the disciples of what appeared to be the last bit they had. As they kept on doing this in implicit obedience, their supply was steadily replenished, whereas had they ceased distributing at any juncture, or stopped short of the last tier of hungry people, the multiplication would have ended abruptly. "There is that scattereth and yet increaseth, and there is that withholdeth more than is meet, but it tendeth to poverty." This rule still holds.

Alas that the Church has to so large an extent lost its original missionary vision, has not kept its eye on the circumference of the circle, "the uttermost part of the earth"! And in the measure in which it has ceased pressing on and out to the whole world, the Lord's blessing has been withheld, and the miracle of His wonder-working power and increase has ceased. One hears of this and that church being financially embarrassed and not being able to make ends meet. We venture to say that on investigation it will be found that those churches have lost, or have never had, the evangelistic and missionary vision and outreach. How can any church claim or expect the Lord's blessing while neglecting the very object for which it was created? What interest has God in helping any church "make ends meet" merely around itself? We have yet to see a truly missionary church struggling for its own financial support. It still remains true that when the Lord's people "seek first the kingdom of God," all these necessary things will be added unto them.

Oh for a fresh, clear, arresting vision of the whole world to break upon the Church of Christ, constraining all Christians to *lift up their eyes* and look out unselfishly beyond their own narrow boundaries and local interests, and share their Saviour's burden of heart for the souls of all mankind! "Where there is no vision, the people perish." How literally and how tragically true that is! Think of the awful fact that nineteen hundred years after Jesus Christ died on the Cross "for the sins of the whole world," hundreds of millions are still living and dying without ever having been told a word about it! Think of those vast solid areas in the hearts of the three missionary continents of Africa, Asia, and South America, where the task of evangelization has not merely to be *finished*, but has at this late date yet to be *begun!* Think of a thousand tribal languages into which not a word of the Book of Life has yet been translated! Nor have the existing missionary forces more than barely touched the fringe of the total need in field after field that we call "occupied." The huge proportions of the unfinished task of missions even in this advanced day are nothing less than staggering, and how anyone who has experienced the blessings of Christ's salvation can view the situation without deep conviction and concern is beyond our understanding. The first great lesson of the parabolic miracle before us is the need of missionary vision.

THE NEED OF COMPASSION

We read that when Jesus lifted up His eyes and beheld the great multitude, "He was moved with compassion toward them." He was not simply touched for the moment with a mild pity of the kind that folks feel when they see some stage play or read a sensational story that gives them a slight shudder and calls forth the ejaculation, "Oh, how dreadful!" but permits them promptly to forget it all in the drive of business or the whirl of pleasure. No, it was anything but that: Jesus was *moved with compassion*. That word "compassion" is a strong word. It literally means "suffering together with," and that is precisely its meaning here as used to describe Jesus' feelings. He actually *suffered* in His compassion for men. His heart bled and broke for sorrowing and sinning humanity. He was called "a man of sorrows and acquainted with grief" because He bore the griefs and carried the sorrows of others, vicariously upon the Cross, we know, but sympathetically also all the way to the Cross. In Isaiah's fine words, "In all their affliction he was afflicted." His compassion stirred the very depths of His soul and moved Him to action. He never shut His heart to any appeal for help.

The statement here about Jesus is repeated in Matthew 9:36 in exactly the same words: "When he saw the multitudes, he was moved with compassion on them," and then the reason for His compassion follows—"because they fainted, and were scattered abroad, as sheep having no shepherd." Note this description of the multitudes as Jesus saw them. *"They fainted"*— from exhaustion, because of burdens too heavy for them to bear. They *"were scattered abroad."* The Greek word is literally *"thrown down,"* and it carries the implication of cruelty or oppression. They were *"as sheep having no shepherd"*—a truly pathetic picture, for sheep are the most helpless and dependent of animals, with no weapon of defense and no instinct of right direction, and therefore they need to be guided, protected, and fed by a kind shepherd.

While the multitudes in the home lands answer this description in some measure, the teeming millions in heathen and Moslem lands do so in a far deeper sense. Indeed, after one has lived in such lands as China and India that word "multitudes" seems to find its full meaning nowhere else. The vision of those surging throngs in the market places and bazaars, at open-air theaters and religious festivals, or as they move in endless procession up and down the city streets can never be effaced. And with what tragic accuracy the language of our text fits their case!

"They faint"—under the crushing burden of dire poverty, the dull drudgery of unremitting toil, the weight of physical affliction unrelieved by any medical or surgical help, and the lack of a hundred features which brighten and bless the homes and communities of Gospel-lighted lands and make life joyous and worth living.

"They are thrown down"—by the forces of injustice, cruelty, and oppression. They are the victims so often of greedy and conscienceless officials who impose upon them crushing taxation and other unrighteous demands. Millions of them have suffered indescribable horrors at the hands of brutal bandits and wicked and unscrupulous enemy forces of invasion. Nor will the story ever be fully told of the anguish and dark despair that hide behind the closed doors of homes where polygamy and domestic slavery reign unchecked.

God's Word declares that "the dark places of the earth are full of the habitations of cruelty," and that "the tender mercies of the wicked are cruel," and how overwhelmingly these statements are confirmed by the actual facts and conditions as seen by a host of reliable witnesses! Slavery, witchcraft, Hindu caste, and opium all continue to take a ghastly toll of lives. It is said that the victims of the African witch doctor's poison cup number 4,000,000 every year. So horrible is life for 27,-000,000 child widows in India that many a little sufferer avails herself of the cover of night to end her miserable existence by a suicidal leap into some deep well. The ravages of opium in China, despite efforts in recent years to banish the cursed drug, still bring physical and moral ruin to countless numbers. These are but a few among a host of open sores in heathendom which cry aloud for healing—a healing which only the Gospel can effect.

"They are as sheep having no shepherd." This word relates pre-eminently to their spiritual destitution, since Jesus Christ is the only Good Shepherd and Saviour of souls. "All that ever came before me," said He, "are thieves and robbers." This, in very truth, defines the religions of the East and of Africa, and their leaders. We make bold so to affirm, despite the misleading report of a self-appointed group of Western "appraisers" who a few years ago, after a tour of inspection of missions in the Far East which was conspicuously superficial, brought back the "verdict" that the ethnic religions are "other ways to God" along with Christianity, and maintained that missionaries should "align themselves with the leaders of the ethnic faiths in a common quest after truth and the ideal way of life." Any intelligent person familiar with these religions in their actual character and working can only attribute such a pronouncement to either pathetic ignorance or shameful dishonesty— unless, indeed, it can be put down to a conception of Christianity utterly different from that which the New Testament presents. For whatever may have been the character and

motive of their founders, these cults as they exist today contain not a vestige of saving grace or power. Their doctrines are false, their practices corrupt, and their leaders are blind leaders of the blind, many of them men of notoriously immoral character, parasites on society, who fleece and victimize the shrine worshipers.

The picture of the multitudes in heathen and Moslem lands is thus a terribly dark and tragic one of temporal misery and degradation, moral turpitude, and spiritual delusion and hopelessness. It is this picture on which the eyes of the Son of man rest as they look down from heaven, and surely no less compassion, but if possible more, fills His heart for these greater multitudes than for those lesser multitudes with whom He mingled in the days of His flesh. Should not every true follower of His share that compassion? Yet there are those who seem utterly to lack this compassion or concern, and who dismiss lightly the case of the heathen with the casual remark, "Oh, but they have their own religions, which are good enough for them." This is but the modern equivalent of the words of the disciples of old, "Send them away, that they may go into the country round about and buy themselves bread." Was this suggestion of theirs a sincere one, think you? We very much fear it was not. For if the country around afforded opportunity of securing food, Jesus as well as His disciples would have been aware of it. No, the suggestion was prompted not by any deep concern for the multitude, but rather by a selfish desire to rid themselves of an unwelcome problem. But observe how the Master thrust back upon them the responsibility they sought to shirk, and sternly replied, "They need not depart; give ye them to eat." And no differently does He reply to the modern descendants of those disciples, who seek to throw off all responsibility for the heathen

today with this flimsy talk about "their own religions" being
"good enough for them." How would these shirkers like to be
bound down by the vile and enslaving rites and customs that
have just been mentioned as attaching to the heathen cults of
today? Would they consider these as "good enough" for themselves? No, the ethnic religions are "good enough" for no one.
The poor souls under their sway have for bread been given a
stone, and for an egg been offered a scorpion. Christ alone is
the Bread of Life, and the Gospel is the only remedy for sin,
whether in America or Asia or Africa. We have this Bread,
this remedy, and our Master is repeating to us those same
words He spoke to His disciples of old: "They need not depart; give ye them to eat."

THE NEED OF CONSECRATED ACTION

Jesus not only *saw*, and *felt;* He also *acted.* Emotion is never
a satisfactory substitute for action. The only compassion that
is real, and that counts, is the compassion that pours itself out
in some material way, in some practical effort for the rescue of
lost souls.

But let us note carefully just *how* He acted, and learn the
lesson it has to teach us. We see Him standing there among
His disciples, His heart beating with desire that they might get
His mind and act with Him. He said to Philip, "Whence shall
we buy bread that these may eat?" There was no uncertainty
in His own mind, but "This he said to prove him; for he himself knew what he would do." Observe that. Jesus was not
embarrassed by the situation, nor is He ever at a loss how to
meet *any* situation. He had a plan *then* to feed those hungry
people, if only His disciples would respond to it and cooperate.
And He has always been fully equal to the problem of world-
evangelization, if only He had full right of way in the hearts

of His people. But how disappointed He must have been when Philip, in the presence of Him who was the Lord of creation, the omnipotent Christ whom he had seen heal the sick and even raise the dead, so utterly failed to reckon on that power, and proceeded to figure out, on a purely human basis, that "two hundred shillings' worth of bread is not sufficient for them, that every one may take a little"!

While not wishing to be too hard on Philip, one cannot refrain from observing what a remarkable discovery his laborious calculations resulted in, namely, that a certain amount of money would *not* be sufficient to give each person in the crowd "a little" (literally "a morsel")—just enough to tickle the palate and increase the sense of hunger without satisfying it. He never reached the point of finding out what sum *would be* sufficient, so that his suggestion was not a positive but only a negative one. At best it was but a poor, temporizing proposal, and as such it stands as a type of the many humanitarian, social, and political schemes which have been devised, and are still being tried, for meeting a world's need. Philip made the fatal mistake of leaving the Lord Jesus out of his calculations, and that same mistake has since been made countless times over, and is still being made today. But no scheme, be it a League of Nations, a World Court, a Peace Conference, or any other organization or structure, howsoever big and imposing, will ever succeed in solving the world's problems while Jesus Christ is not recognized and His principles and power are ignored. They are all doomed to failure.

In the incident before us, Andrew is next mentioned. He came nearer to Jesus' thought when he said: "There is a lad here, which hath five barley loaves, and two small fishes." True, he nearly spoiled this hopeful suggestion by adding, "but what are they among so many?" However, the Lord brushed aside this unfortunate "but," and promptly gave the word, "Make the men sit down,"—which was as much as to say, "You've hit the mark, Andrew. Now let's get to work." Why do we draw this conclusion? We do so because it has always been the divine way to work through human instruments, and Andrew's introduction of the little lad was in keeping with this plan. Men are ever seeking methods, but God is seeking men. In His wonderful economy He has graciously chosen to associate men with Himself, and to use the human factor in the working out of the divine purpose. He deigned that day to use the little lad and his tiny supply of food as His medium of feeding that great crowd. Jesus and the lad cooperated and did the job together. If someone objects to this statement and protests that Jesus could have done it without the lad, our answer is simply that He *did not* do it without him. It was unquestionably Jesus' power that wrought that mighty miracle, but it was just as truly the lad's lunch through which that power wrought.

Now that little lad stands out as an example of consecration. Who was this lad? How did he come to be there? Were the loaves and fishes a lunch which had been prepared for his own use? Or were they possibly goods he had for sale? All these questions have been made a matter of much speculative comment. But the Word gives us no answer to any of them, and therefore we do not know, or need to know. What we *do* know is that "Jesus took the loaves" of the lad, and with them fed the multitude. And what we may be assured of is that Jesus did not arbitrarily appropriate the boy's loaves: that would not have been like Jesus. The boy must have offered them to Jesus, and He accepted them.

What a never-to-be-forgotten day that was for the lad! Little did he dream, as he started out that morning to hear the great preacher, what the day would hold for him. But the golden opportunity faced him of giving what he had to the Lord Jesus; he responded and gave it, and the Lord Jesus accepted his gift, multiplied it by His divine power, and made it the means of supplying the need of more than five thousand hungry people. How impressive it all is—and the more so as we reflect upon the alternative choice the lad might have made! He might have held on to his loaves and fishes for his own use, as most folks would undoubtedly have done. But that would have meant merely satisfying his appetite for a few hours, and then he would have passed on and nothing would ever have been heard of him. Happily he chose the better course of yielding the little that he had to the Lord, and thereby becoming a partner with Him in ministering to the need of a multitude of others. As he witnessed the result of his action that day, and as the memory of it lingered on through the days and years that followed, what joy and satisfaction must have been his, in the thought of having been thus used by the Omnipotent Christ, and to the blessing of his fellow men!

Nor did the record of the lad and his loaves end with that one day, for the story has been told to every generation since, and the whole world over, and countless men and women have been moved by it to offer their lives and their substance to the same Lord, as loaves to be broken and multiplied by His almighty power to the feeding of earth's multitudes starving for the Bread of Life. Well do we recall how the incident of the little lad came home to our own heart in early youth with conviction and inspiration, and led to life surrender and dedication to the One who, once the Man of Galilee, is now the Christ of glory, to be used wherever and however He saw fit for the carrying of His redemptive message to a lost world. Scores of names of others known to us come readily to mind, who were similarly moved to follow the little lad's example in placing themselves at the Master's disposal for this same purpose. In every case He took the proffered gift, however much or little, and multiplied it an hundredfold to the saving of many precious souls, and to the spiritual enrichment of the giver beyond all words to express.

The long list recorded in Scripture of *little* people, and *little* things, that God was pleased to use as His chosen instruments is truly impressive. We think of "the child Samuel" as God's mouthpiece to Eli the priest. We think of David, the youngest of all Jesse's sons but preferred by the Lord above his brethren, and recall how later on he slew the giant warrior Goliath "with a sling and with a stone." We think of Gideon, who pleaded that "my family is the poorest in Manasseh, and I am the least in my father's house," and of his putting to rout the mighty host of Midian with a paltry force of three hundred men armed with trumpets and empty pitchers. And then there were also the "little maid" who told the "great man" Naaman of Syria about the true God and thus brought him healing for his leprosy, and the widow of Zarephath whose "little oil in a cruse" was God's means of sustaining the life of Elijah the prophet for many days. Shamgar's "ox goad" too, and Samson's "jawbone of an ass" were other insignificant "little things" which God deigned to use. Nor can we ever forget the "little colt" which bore Jesus on His triumphal ride into Jerusalem. Moreover, these are to be regarded not as exceptions to God's usual mode of working but rather as typical instances of it, even as His Word tells us that "God hath chosen the foolish things . . . and the weak things . . . and base things . . . and things that are despised" as His preferred instruments for use, to the end "that no flesh should glory in his presence" (I Cor. 1:27).

What encouragement is thus held out to those among the

Lord's people who may have fewer talents or more slender means to offer Him for His service! Missionary annals are full of instances of men and women who were born in humble homes, grew up with meager advantages, and at the outset of their missionary careers gave promise of being only ordinary "rank and file" material, but who in service with and for Christ developed marvelously and rose to lofty heights. One has only to mention as illustrations William Carey the cobbler, Robert Morrison the boot-last maker, David Livingstone the cotton spinner, and Mary Slessor the poor factory girl, all of whose names now stand out conspicuously among the greatest missionary names in history. "Little is much when God is in it."

We know of nothing more awe-inspiring than the fact revealed in Scripture, and illustrated in the incident before us, that the Lord has made man necessary to Himself in the accomplishment of His great purposes in the world. The thought is not that man was inherently necessary, but only that God in His sovereignty chose to make him necessary. As has already been said, Jesus *could* have fed the multitude without the little lad, but He *chose not to do so*. To express the same thought in a different way, and employing other Scriptural imagery which sets forth the relation of believers to Christ in this Church age as still more close and vital than that of the little lad in his day, we turn to two familiar New Testament metaphors. First, Jesus said, "I am the vine, ye are the branches." Now we well know that the branch needs the vine as the essential source of its very life. But it is also true that the vine needs the branches, for only through them does the vine bear its fruit. Then also the figure of the body is used, of which Christ is the head and believers are the members. That figure expresses the profound truth of the organic unity of all true Christians with Him. They are vitally and inseparably joined to Him, actually a part of Him. It follows conclusively that just as the head of our human body can carry out its will and purpose only through the response and cooperation of its various members, even so Christ, the glorious Head of the Church which is His Body, can carry out His gracious desire and design for mankind only as the members of that Body yield themselves to become the instruments through which He can work unhindered and effectually. In His missionary enterprise some members must be His eyes to see, others His feet to go, His tongue to speak, His hands to serve. The following lines give expression to this thought:

> Thou hast no tongue, O Christ, as once of old,
> To tell the story of Thy love divine;
> The story still the same, as sweet, as true,
> But there's no tongue to tell it out but mine.
>
> Thou hast no hands, O Christ, as once of old,
> To feed the multitude with bread divine;
> Thou hast the Living Bread, enough for all,
> But there's no hand to give it out but mine.
>
> Thou hast no feet, O Christ, as once to go
> Where Thy lost sheep in sorrow pine;
> Thy love is still the same, as deep, as true,
> But now Thou hast no feet to go but mine.
>
> And shall I use these ransomed powers of mine
> For things that only minister to me?
> Lord, take my tongue, my hands, my heart, my all,
> And let me live, and love, and give for Thee.

The lesson the Lord Jesus would teach His followers today through this missionary parable of the feeding of the five thousand is unmistakably clear. He *chose to need* that little lad to be His partner in that miracle of mercy. He waited for his offer of the loaves and fishes, and He manifested His divine power, not independently but *through that yielded offering*.

Similarly He *has chosen to need* those who today are His pledged disciples, to be His willing partners in the work of giving His Gospel to the whole world. "Ye SHALL be my witnesses . . . unto the uttermost part of the earth."

Christ needs some to GO. It is a high honor and priceless privilege to be His ambassador, His witness, to benighted peoples beyond the seas. It far transcends all other callings, and is the grandest life investment ever offered to men.

Christ needs all to GIVE—for *all* can give *something*, even although not all in the same measure. What a comfort it should be to those who cannot go in person that they may still have a part by giving, in order that others may go! Would that many more of God's children might catch the higher vision of money, as not merely something to cater to selfish pleasure and adornment, but something to invest in winning souls as gems for the crown of *His* adornment in the glorious day of His appearing!

Christ needs all to PRAY. The Lord is said to have "wondered that there was no intercessor." He must still wonder that there are not many more intercessors, when the way to the Throne of Grace has been paved as it is with marvelous prayer promises. The prophet Isaiah's sad complaint to God was that "there is none that stirreth up himself to take hold of thee." Doors in certain mission fields at times close temporarily for preaching, but the door to the Throne-room of heaven never closes for this holiest and mightiest form of missionary service, and the one in which *all*, not merely some, may share. Oh for more Christians who will "give themselves to prayer," and thus "move the hand that moves the world, to bring salvation down."

We offer one further word in conclusion. The account of the distribution of the loaves recorded in Matthew's Gospel

(14:19) reads: "He blessed, and brake, and gave the loaves to his disciples, and the disciples to the multitude." Three words stand out—LOAVES, DISCIPLES, MULTITUDE: observe them carefully, and their order and relation. Now where do we find the disciples? They are between the loaves and the multitude. How did the loaves get to the multitude? They were distributed through the disciples, and only thus, for Jesus did not Himself give them directly to the multitude, but by the hands of the disciples. Just here lies a vitally important truth in this parable of missions. When the blessed Son of God came down to earth from the glory He took upon Himself the burden of responsibility for a lost world. He went resolutely to the Cross and there offered Himself as an atoning sacrifice for the sins of the world. "It is finished!" was His triumphant cry as He died. Then He rose from the dead and returned to heaven. But just before He left for the glory, He summoned that little charter group of disciples around Him on Olivet and gave to them what we call the Great Commission. He said to them in effect: "My brethren, I have done My part by providing Salvation for the whole world. Now your part is to carry this Message of Salvation to every creature, to be My witnesses unto the uttermost part of the earth." In other words, and employing the language of our missionary parable, the risen Christ placed in His disciples' hands the "loaves," the Bread of Life, for the perishing "multitude" of mankind. He transferred to them the responsibility that had rested until then upon Him.

That responsibility to tell the whole world of the Saviour has been passed on from one generation of Christians to another, and today it is ours. We stand, as those disciples of old, between the loaves and the multitude, and that in one of two ways: either as obstructionists, withholding the loaves from

the multitude by our indifference, selfishness, and sloth; or else
as Christ's loyal helpers, passing out the loaves from His hands
to the multitude. We must find our place in one or other of
these two categories: there is no third. May this solemn truth
search the conscience and move the heart of every reader, convicting of the duty, and persuading of the high privilege, of
fulfilling the sacred trust committed to the Church, and to
every individual member of that Church, of taking the Bread
of Life with all possible speed to a multitude of souls that are
dying for the lack of it.

> "Lord, Thou hast giv'n to me a trust,
>   A high and holy dispensation,
> To tell the world, and tell I must,
>   The story of Thy great salvation;
> Thou might'st have sent from heav'n above
>   Angelic hosts to tell the story,
> But in Thy condescending love,
>   On men Thou hast conferred the glory.
>
> "Let me be faithful to my trust,
>   Telling the world the story;
> Press on my heart the woe,
>   Put in my feet the go;
> Let me be faithful to my trust,
>   And use me for Thy glory."